THE
NEW
JOURNALISM

THE
NEW
JOURNALISM

The Underground Press,
the Artists of
Nonfiction,
and Changes in
the Established Media

by Michael L. Johnson

The University Press of Kansas/Lawrence/Manhattan/Wichita

Acknowledgments

I am grateful to the University of Kansas for a summer grant from the General Research Fund which gave me the time to write, to Douglas Milburn who made me pay attention to what was happening, to my mother and father who helped me believe in the possibility of bridging the gaps between people, to the staff of the University Press of Kansas who have been of great help to a young writer, and to many other friends whose comments and life-styles made the writing of this book a necessary and meaningful act. Grateful acknowledgment is made to the following for permission to quote excerpts from their material:

The Algiers Motel Incident, by John Hersey. Copyright © 1968 by John Hersey; published by Alfred A. Knopf, Inc., pages 30, 33-34 (hardcover edition).
Allen Ginsberg in America, by Jane Kramer. Copyright © 1968, 1969 by Jane Kramer; published by Random House, Inc.
The Armies of the Night, by Norman Mailer. Copyright © 1968 by Norman Mailer; reprinted by permission of the World Publishing Company from *The Armies of the Night* by Norman Mailer, an NAL book.
The Black Panthers, by Gene Marine. Copyright © 1969 by Gene Marine; published by The New American Library.
"The Conventions, 1968," by Peter Shaw, reprinted from *Commentary*, December 1968, by permission. Copyright © 1968 by the American Jewish Committee.
Death at An Early Age, by Jonathan Kozol. Copyright © 1967 by Jonathan Kozol; copyright © 1967 by The New York Times Company; published by Houghton Mifflin Company.
"Double Perspective on Hysteria," by Robert Scholes in *Saturday Review*, 24 August 1968. Copyright © 1968 by Saturday Review, Inc.
The Electric Kool-Aid Acid Test, by Tom Wolfe. Copyright © 1968 by Tom Wolfe; reprinted with the permission of Farrar, Straus & Giroux, Inc.
Famous Long Ago: My Life and Hard Times with Liberation News Service, by Raymond Mungo. Copyright © 1970 by Raymond Mungo; reprinted by permission of Beacon Press.

To Lee Ann...

who is patient

Contents

Introduction   xi

1   A Short History of the Underground Press:
Beginnings and Growth   1

2   The Expansion of the Underground Press   23

3   Three Major Stylists: Truman Capote,
Tom Wolfe, and Norman Mailer   43

4   New Journalists Writing on the General Scene
and the Race and War Scene   85

5   Other New Journalists: The Youth and Radical
Scene and the New Muckrakers   117

6   Hopeful Signs and Conclusions   147

Notes   153

Index   167

Introduction

Gone with the wind. Hosts at Mullaghmast
and Tara of the kings. Miles of ears of
porches. The tribune's words howled and
scattered to the four winds. A people
sheltered within his voice. Dead noise. Akasic
records of all that ever anywhere wherever
was. Love and laud him: me no more.

Stephen Dedalus
in James Joyce's *Ulysses*

In the term "New Journalism" I am using the word
journalism to signify both "journalistic writing" as it is found
in books, newspapers, and magazines, and, in the broader
meaning of the word, "editorial practice" or the "publishing or
broadcasting of journalistic material." New Journalism, as the
term is popularly used, usually refers to the writing of a new
class of journalists, including such people as Tom Wolfe and
Norman Mailer, who have broken away from traditional journalistic practice to exercise the freedom of a new subjective,
creative, and candid style of reportage and commentary.[1] That
meaning of the term is generally accurate, and it covers also
the writers of the underground press, who are themselves New
Journalists, though generally not such good ones as Mailer and
Wolfe. Furthermore, that meaning is very helpful in deciding
which journalists fall under the heading of New Journalists and
which do not. However, I think, for the purpose of discussing
New Journalism and its context fully, it is necessary to expand
the definition of the term to include other aspects of journalism,

such as the underground press as an evolving institution, rock journalism, underground radio, and what I call New Muckraking, so that it is possible to speak of a whole pattern of change in journalism during the 1960's. This approach necessarily includes some consideration of conventional or established journalism, implicitly or explicitly, as background, as well as some sociological and political commentary. Nonetheless, as popular usage of the term suggests, it is the writing itself—its style and technique, its expression of the writer as a person, and its record of human events—that is central, and it is to the writing that I will give my closest attention.

New Journalism, as we shall see, differs in many important ways from established journalism; but it also involves a realization of many of the neglected possibilities of its established, traditional counterpart, and at its best it involves a renewed commitment to principles of honesty and thoroughness that should be part of any good journalism. This realization and commitment have come about most markedly during the 1960's, particularly since 1965. It is clear that parallel to the revolutionary changes in our whole environment during the 1960's is a radical transformation in journalism, a transformation which has been effected both through its responding to those changes and, more significantly, through its aiding in their implementation. Journalism has always responded to changes in man's political, social, and technological environment, and it has always taken an attitude either of an assumed objectivity or of a selective affirmation or opposition toward those changes, in terms of all the biases that can command the media. However, during the 1960's these changes have been so fast and profound, and their calling for moral attitudes and understanding so loud, that conscientious journalism has metamorphosed itself in an attempt to be relevant and to participate communicatively in those changes. This journalism has thus evolved, by quick quantum leaps, into a New Journalism.

As Marshall McLuhan has been pointing out for years: in order to understand an environment, one must somehow transcend the kinds of consciousness that confine him within it; thus, with a new form of consciousness, he may see more clearly, with new eyes. At the same time, however, one must participate critically in the flow of human events. New Journalism has, in one degree or another, assumed a sort of "outlaw" attitude in order to fulfill McLuhan's dictum, and it has moved beyond the generally rigid attitudes of the established media and yet stayed very close to the events it reports. Through its new consciousness and its new language it has communicated fresher and more helpful information about the changes occurring in our world, and in one way or another it has proven more thorough, more honest, and more intelligently critical than traditional journalism.

The shortcomings of traditional journalistic practice have been pointed out continuously and voluminously during the last few years. There has been a plethora of books exposing the media's promotion rather than criticism of governmental policy, its inability to respond sensitively to the problems and alienation of black Americans, its commitment to sensationalizing change rather than communicating understanding of it, and its failure to persevere in the careful articulation of truth rather than rhetorical claims, hearsay, and prejudice. For example, Ben H. Bagdikian, a Washington press critic, points out that

> too many news organizations see their job as doing no more than transmitting information that comes most easily over the transom. Few have the competence to understand the systems of government and business they should monitor. And, lastly, too many are so close to officialdom that they are defensive about its performance. News organizations too devoted to the status quo resist evidence that the status quo isn't working. For too many news operations in too many communities the official, bureaucratic view of the world is the press view of the world.[2]

For anyone who reads the popular press, watches television, or listens to radio with awareness, this must seem axiomatic for most of what he experiences.

The riots in black ghettos during the mid-1960's gave rise to a flood of studies concerning the role of the media, not only as to how they reported those riots but also as to how they caused them. Their coverage was generally sensationalistic and ignorant, and there is no end to stories of reporters or television cameramen encouraging rioters' activities in order to "make a good story." The problem of coverage is related to a larger fact: the established media in America are both consciously and unconsciously racist and in some cases blatantly racially bigoted. According to Jack Lyle, a University of California professor of journalism,

> In terms of the usual operational criterion for news selection . . . , little has been happening in the Negro areas. Economically, these are the most stagnant areas of our cities . . . . Politically, minority groups have been the most apathetic segments of the population and it is only in recent years that candidates and political writers have shown awareness of "the Negro vote." The centers of cultural activity are generally elsewhere. Even Negro crime tends to be ignored. Crime is such an everyday, everywhere occurrence that it is news only when prominent persons are involved or it is carried out on a particularly large scale or in an unusual manner. Traditionally, then, Negro areas have not been considered newsworthy. Reporters rarely ventured into the Negro ghetto, rarely wrote of its problems. Thus it was easy for the majority of the population to plead ignorance of these problems.[3]

This problem must seem clear once it is stated and recognized, and so must the fact that the established media's avoidance of the ghetto derives from a perverse set of priorities concerning the purposes of journalism.

The established media's sensationalizing of "newsworthy" information and their failure in the evaluation of truth are by now common knowledge, and these factors have contributed to the so-called "credibility gap" that is widening into a national abyss. Speaking specifically of the press, Bill Moyers, former presidential press secretary and later publisher of *Newsday*, states the case humorously and poignantly:

> I learned at the White House that of all the great myths of American journalism, objectivity is the greatest. . . . "The disbelief in the press is a national joke. . . . There is little public trust today." . . . It is a sad reflection on the state of our reputation today that far more readers believe the advice they get from Ann Landers than they do the advice of our editorials.[4]

Considering this statement and those cited previously, one begins to see all at once the limitations of the established media and their journalistic character. Had they the necessary intelligence and adaptability, they might have saved our era from its incredible violence and fearfulness by creating a truly informed public. As it is, they have failed spectacularly.

I would argue that it is New Journalism, growing slowly during the 1960's into its own voice, learning from the errors of its parents (like its generally youthful writers and promoters), that has created, if only on a minority scale, a more intelligent, actively concerned, and informed public to counter that of the established media. I think it has overcome many of its parents' errors and has exercised a freedom of informative expression not to be found at any other time or place in the world. That is not to say that it is without faults, because it has its own; and its expression is not totally free or wholly informed, because its freedom has been constrained in some ways and its information distorted by virtue of its humanity and its own kinds of bias. But it has succeeded far better than its traditional counterpart, if as yet only a limited basis, in trying to present to the American public a full picture of its world.

What then, specifically, constitutes the New Journalism? I am concerned, as I said earlier, primarily with written journalism, although much of what I will have to say is relevant also for television and radio. In assembling and discussing material which somehow exemplifies the idea of New Journalism, I have tried to keep an open mind as to what the term includes and to allow the material itself to form the boundaries of a definition. I have regarded virtually any observably significant change in journalism during the last decade as having potential bearing on the development of a new set of journalistic attitudes, practices, and styles, and I have tried to select material which clearly shows the most relevant and dramatic of those changes.

There are, it seems to me, three large categories of New Journalism which have developed in the 1960's: 1) the underground press and publications closely related to it; 2) books or essays written in a journalistic style by journalists and, perhaps more significantly, by people inside and outside the fields of literary endeavor who have formulated a direct, evaluative, and, usually, participative response to events in their world by using or inventing a journalistic voice; 3) changes in the established media that involve significantly different and fresh journalistic approaches to reportage of and commentary upon the events with which they concern themselves.

The papers and magazines of the underground press may be found on college campuses, in bookstores, and on street corners across the country, the most articulate and informative being publications such as the Los Angeles *Free Press,* the *East Village Other* from New York, and the *Avatar* from Boston. Examples of New Journalistic books are: *The Kandy-Kolored Tangerine-Flake Streamline Baby* by Tom Wolfe, at the time of the book's publication a journalist for the New York *Herald Tribune; The Black Panthers* by Gene Marine, a senior editor of *Ramparts* magazine; *Miami and the Siege of Chicago* by Norman Mailer, a novelist and part-time journalist turned full-time journalist; and *The Strawberry Statement: Notes of a College Revolutionary* by James Kunen, a student at Columbia University. Examples of changes in the established media may be seen in the fact that much of the material in the second category is published in such magazines as *Harper's* or the *Atlantic,* in the gradual "liberalizing" of some newspapers, in the rise of an underground radio network, and in television's gradual broadening of journalistic reportage and opinion—exemplary programs being Sander Vanocur's *First Tuesday* or specials on ecology, drugs, and so forth, and NET's admirable programs concerning American youth, like *America, Inc.*

Let me, then, turn to the New Journalism.

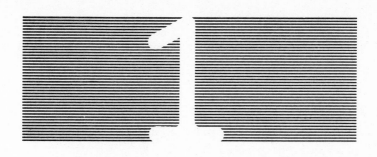

A SHORT HISTORY OF
THE UNDERGROUND PRESS:
BEGINNINGS
AND
GROWTH

> The editors of the new journalism see themselves as reeducating American youth and unifying and solidifying the revolutionary movement. The Underground press is not just reporting on, but making a revolution.
>
> Naomi Feigelson,
> *The Underground Revolution:*
> *Hippies, Yippies, and Others*

In 1948 Paul F. Lazarsfeld and Robert K. Merton were very much aware of the dynamics of the mass media, and they noted three of their central social functions: the "status-conferral function," whereby the media confer status upon and legitimize the authority of individuals, organizations, and movements (thus, ironically, Lee Harvey Oswald became a kind of national "hero" through the media); the "enforcement of social norms," whereby the rhetoric of the media defines and controls the character of social behavior; the "narcotizing dysfunction," the public paralysis attendant upon a flood of media information which is too large in dosage to be translated into useful attitudes or actions, so that knowing the news, having knowledge of events, no matter how condensed and distorted, comes to be identified with reacting to them and *doing* something about them.[1] It is undoubtedly true that these three functions of media have acted in such a way as to create a rigid public, although there may be a certain token elasticity within the boundaries of its rigidity. The complacent conformity one associates with the 1950's or the silent-majority mentality one associates with the 1960's are creations, in large part, of these media functions. They have helped to produce a stifling human environment in this country, and they have supported the powers that maintain that environment.

A Short History of the Underground Press

The underground press, more directly and noisily than any other organ of the New Journalism, has become a force opposing these functions and the society they have influenced. In a journalistic style that includes deep personal sincerity, concern, and sensitivity, as well as militant near-illiteracy, it has attempted to raise a voice that will be heard clearly on a different plane from the established media and that will, by its distinctiveness, avoid the narcotizing dysfunction and offer practical possibilities for awakening and acting socially, politically, ecologically. This voice is the most revolutionary and, to those alienated from its audience, shocking that has ever been raised against the status quo and for a new way of life and communication.

Ben H. Bagdikian has called for "a new form of American journalism: The regular presentation of proposed solutions to leading problems by thoughtful men outside of journalism."[2] Most of the people involved in the underground press *are* radically outside of established journalism. Although there are some renegade journalists involved in the running of these presses, most of their people have learned or, rather, created their journalism as they went along; and most of the presses could not operate without the devotion of people who work for little or no salary. They are motivated fundamentally by principle, not income, and this is the secret of their legitimacy, not-easy success, and, especially, their independence.

I. F. Stone, a man who is also in many ways "outside journalism" and a founding father of the underground ethos, has published his *I. F. Stone's Weekly* in Washington steadily since January 1953. A voice of political sanity from the McCarthy era to the present, he places great stress on the need for journalistic independence. He claims that he is even one up on Ben Franklin, because he does not accept advertising. The story of his success suggests a basic journalistic credo for the underground press:

> My idea was to make the Weekly radical in viewpoint but conservative in format. I picked a beautiful typeface, Garamond, for my main body type, and eschewed traditional headlines. I made no claim to inside stuff—obviously a radical reporter in those days [early 1950's] had few pipelines into the government. I tried to give information which could be documented so the reader

could check it for himself. I tried to dig the truth out of hearings, official transcripts and government documents, and to be as accurate as possible. I also sought to give the Weekly a personal flavor, to add humor, wit and good writing to the Weekly report. I felt that if one were able enough and had sufficient vision one could distill meaning, truth and even beauty from the swiftly flowing debris of the week's news. I sought in political reporting what Galsworthy in another context called the "significant trifle" —the bit of dialogue, the overlooked fact, the buried observation which illuminated the realities of the situation. These I often used in "boxes" to lighten up the otherwise solid pages of typography unrelieved either by picture or advertising. I tried in every issue to provide fact and opinion not available elsewhere in the press.[3]

The underground newspapers of the 1960's, in contrast, have been generally dependent on some advertising, but Stone's conception of the maverick reporter as a conscientious muckraker with the sensibility of Galsworthy or Henry James for the unreported detail or the hidden side of events is one which is relevant for much of the best underground journalism. And although the underground presses have access to more information than Stone did during the early life of the *Weekly*, they still maintain a critical independence of their sources, the government, and the established press. They have their own reporters, and most of the presses are associated with one or both of two underground syndicates, the Liberation News Service or the Underground Press Syndicate, which distribute news and other journalistic writing. Furthermore, most of their advertisers are closely aligned with their views, so that they worry little about the withdrawal of advertising money; and many of the larger papers make a tidy income with personal and classified want ads, all the way from motorcycles to sell to sexual services offered—and the ads tend to solidify the public which they are addressing and act, with the letters to the editor, as a sort of forum for the paper's audience.

Most underground newspapers attempt to be a real tribune and an informative voice for the community of people they represent. Their independence, financial and otherwise, gives them a context of freedom in which to operate. Their independence and freedom are their strength as a journalistic medium and as a voice of dissent. This distinguishes them significantly from most established newspapers and the media in general. Again, I. F. Stone is helpful:

> The fault I find with most American newspapers is not the absence of dissent. It is the absence of news. With a dozen or so honorable exceptions, most American newspapers carry very little news. Their main concern is advertising. The main interest of our society is merchandising. All the so-called communications industries are primarily concerned not with communications, but with selling. This is obvious on television and radio but it is only a little less obvious in the newspapers. Most owners of newspapers are businessmen, not newspapermen. The news is something which fills the spaces left over by the advertisers. The average publisher is not only hostile to dissenting opinion, he is suspicious of *any* opinion likely to antagonize any reader or consumer.[4]

What Stone says is obviously true for most established newspapers. Furthermore, when those newspapers do present real news, it is usually bad news—as Marshall McLuhan says, "real news is 'bad' news." The underground press to some extent has fallen into this trap also, but it is in general more genuinely affirmative of the life-styles it promotes than the established press is of those to which it pays lip service by the profit motive. That is to say, the good news of the underground press is more honest, and there is no social-climbing claptrap. Furthermore, its tolerance for opinion is virtually infinite compared to that of the established press, and even its bad news tends to be more detailed and informative.

The reportage of the underground press is also independent or taken from LNS or UPS, both of which also operate independently. According to John Wilcock, formerly a reporter for the New York *Daily Mirror* and now a hit-and-run underground editor,

> In the area of reporting, the underground press has shown singular audacity in digging up its own facts, getting its own fads going, and creating its own mythology. While the establishment papers moronically or insidiously accept every body count, government snow job and press agent puffery that comes in over the wire, the underground press

relies on men from Vietnam, empirical evidence on the streets and in the ghettos, and personal confrontation.[5]

This idealistic, and, I think, generally true statement should be taken with a small grain of salt, though, because the anger and prejudices of underground-press reportage can sometimes make it just as bigoted and valueless as that of the established press. Nonetheless, most of the time the underground tries programmatically to be more thorough than its counterparts feeding off AP and UPI.

In the mid-1950's of I. F. Stone there was really only one truly underground newspaper in the country, a Greenwich Village weekly called the *Village Voice*, whereas there are now around 300.[6] Until the early and mid-1960's the *Voice* was the only regularly published paper of strong dissenting views, besides Stone's *Weekly* and a few lesser, politically liberal papers. Norman Mailer, who has since become one of the most articulate New Journalists, helped found the *Voice* as a weekly in 1955 with editor Dan Wolf and publisher Ed Fancher. Several months after its founding Mailer began writing a column for the *Voice*, trying to give it direction. His attacks on the community of the Village earned him a reputation as a controversy-provoking journalist and did not help the paper's being accepted sympathetically. The *Voice* did not show a profit until eight years later when the underground impulse began to grow more powerful. It has never been as loud and radical an organ of dissent and far-out life-styles as Mailer wanted it to be, and his friction with the editors was rough enough that his column ended after eighteen issues. In retrospect he is very much aware of the differences between his and their conceptions of the paper:

> "They wanted it to be successful; I wanted it to be outrageous. They wanted a newspaper that could satisfy the conservative community—church news, meeting of political organizations, so forth. I believed we could grow only if we tried to reach an audience in which no newspaper had yet been interested. I had the feeling of an underground revolution on its way, and I do not know that I was wrong."[7]

He might well have added that he wanted a new kind of newspaper for an audience that had as yet been interested in few newspapers, because it has been one of the functions of the underground to create a new acceptance of the newspaper as a medium.

Looking back, one can see that Mailer was right, that since the *Voice*, which has remained conservative compared to its progeny, an underground revolution has occurred; and most of the papers caught in that revolution have followed, roughly speaking, the radical direction proposed by his columns. Nonetheless, even though in many ways conservative and successful (circulation is now around 150,000), the *Voice* is still the paper that opened the frontier of the underground:

> By avoiding the peculiar preoccupations of the true underground, the *Village Voice's* circulation rose from 20,000 to 75,000 in the past three years [from 1964-1967]— with one quarter of its papers sold outside the metropolitan area. . . . It is still decidedly a community newspaper— embroiled in local skirmishes for reform Democrats, schools, zoning laws—but it judged early in the game that Greenwich Village was not a community like any other. Rather it billeted, in remarkably close quarters, much of the vanguard of American fashion, art, politics and theater and was, therefore, worthy of representation of the world "out there." . . . *Voice* reporters lived their beats; covering civil rights, off-Broadway, the Pop scene or a neighborhood campaign, they wrote, essentially, about themselves and about their friends. When they broadened their sights, they tended—where the *Nation, Commonweal* or *New Leader* sounded faintly old, tired and square—to be in touch with what was happening. And so the *Voice*, bolstered by almost weekly gains in advertising, shows signs of becoming the first national organ for insurgency in politics and the arts.
>
> The *Voice* opened up the territory. The papers that moved in to occupy it were, in one sense, children of the radical mimeo sheets and, in another, children of the *Voice*. Some were promising, some were mentally defective. But all reacted against the conservatism of their *Voice* parent; they swore at birth enmity to compromise.[8]

Even though it is now scorned as "liberal" by the newer underground papers, the *Voice* was and still is a paper worth reading; and it was partly responsible for the development of many good New Journalists, such as Richard Goldstein, now editor of the underground magazine *US*, Michael Harrington, and Nat Hentoff, among others. Furthermore, though it is politically liberal, it has given very conscientious coverage to much radical political activity, and it is a dependable source of news concerning rock music, film, and avant garde or underground artistic activity. It has, in its own way, kept in touch.

Besides the successful *Voice* there were a few other underground publications during the 1950's. Most of these were clearly political in their journalism and did not develop the broader concerns and subject matter of the more recent papers. There was a good deal of satire and general debunking in addition to reportage, though. Besides *I. F. Stone's Weekly*, there were, for example: M. S. Arnoni's *Minority of One*, a serious journal concerned with such looming questions as nuclear holocaust, the cold war, and the possibilities of pacifism; Lyle Stuart's *The Independent*, which was consistently devoted to putting down Christianity and the idiocies of censorship; Victor Navasky's *Monocle*, which was lighter and satirical; and more maverick, satire-oriented publications, such as *Aardvark* from Chicago and *Horseshit* from California's "Scum Press."

These papers, with the *Voice*, prepared ground for the *Realist*, begun in 1958 by Paul Krassner, an ex-comedian and raving sexual prophet-satirist. The *Realist*, perhaps more than any other publication before the mid-1960's, demonstrated the forms of journalistic freedom and style to be developed by the underground. Jacob Brackman describes it as

> a hippie-dippie urban marriage of *I. F. Stone's Weekly*, *Confidential* and *Mad*. Almost from the beginning, the Magazine of Irreverence, Applied Paranoia, Rural Naïveté, Neuter Gender, Criminal Negligence, Egghead Junkies (Krassner kept changing his mind on the masthead) abounded in wit and style. Krassner demonstrated that literacy was not tantamount to squareness. *"The Realist,"* commented one New York writer with considerable glee, "is the *Village Voice* with its fly open."⁹

The description is apt, for Krassner's expansion of the underground's concerns was primarily toward the inclusion of more sexual matter. Sex and politics, the subjects with which most popular publications are concerned in one degree of sublimation and displacement or another, were desublimated and put naked on center stage in the *Realist*. Everything within this double constellation of events came into play, and Krassner's debt to *Mad*, in many ways an archetypal underground magazine, and the *Confidential*-ilk of magazines is unmistakable. There was, and still is, a tabloid aspect to the *Realist*, and it has its own kind of put-on sensationalism. Krassner eventually pushed Mailer's dream about as far toward the edge as it could go, writing imaginatively and, to the typical popular mind, obscenely, about abortion, censorship, and a multitude of other exposés and put-on's, part informatively factual, behind the scenes, part tongue-in-cheek.

The *Realist* was undoubtedly one of the most important experiments in underground journalism, and it is still an inspired and entertaining publication; but it has failed to be a full voice for the audience it commands, which is now in excess of a quarter of a million. Its political news is still not reliable, and it seems in some ways more devoted to being a parody of the popular press than to improving upon it. In its beginning the paper was too radical to reach a very large audience, not only because of local censorship but also because a large public for Krassner's antics did not yet exist. The *Realist* was founded in the Eisenhower era, and the cracks in the political-social structure and in America's sexual rigidity were not yet dramatically visible. It was an easy and somnolent time compared to the 1960's, and that fact limited the audience of the *Realist*, the *Voice*, and their peer publications as well as tempering any tendencies away from conservatism. It was a time before the information explosion, sexual openness, and political activism of the 1960's.

The forces which galvanized the 1960's as an environment for the New Journalism and the rise of the underground press are various and complex and, for the most part, have been reduced through popular philosophy to rhetorical clichés. Furthermore, because of their rapid development, it is difficult to evaluate the character of their interactions with one another. However, there are certain motions of these forces which should be seen in perspective. The election of John Kennedy to the presidency in 1960 was clearly a promise for the youthful flowering of the complacent hopes of the 1950's. The first part of the 1960's seems in retrospect to have been a free ride on the energies of the previous decade, under the guidance of a man who was a symbol of beauty, strength, and idealism. I would suggest, as many others have, that it was his assassination in November of 1963 that really marked the beginning of a cultural and political revolution—certainly not his election three years earlier. The shock of his death wore off slowly, the disillusionment more slowly still.

Whatever the symbolic overtones of Kennedy's assassination were, the immediate effect was to install Lyndon Johnson and his administration. The international and domestic policies of Johnson's government served as a catalyst to radicalize the cultural attitudes of many American people, particularly the young, who were sick of the Vietnam war, the country's entrenched racism, bigotry, and complacency, the inequities of the draft, and a hundred other kinds of funk and oppression that seemed to control their lives and the lives of anyone else in the world who was within reach of a bureaucratic official. Out of this radicalization grew what Theodore Roszak, in his *The Making of a Counter Culture: Reflections on the Technocratic Society and Its Youthful Opposition* (New York: Doubleday & Co., Inc., 1969), calls the counterculture: an aggregate of persons, ideologies, and activities, politically left, technologically conservative, that constitutes an alternative culture opposed to the mainstream of technocratic progress and the dominance of the present educational-governmental-social system. That counterculture has confronted and exposed the cynicism and brutality of the dominant American culture directly and with intellectually articulate criticism. Its people have also attempted all manner of experiments in alternative and radical life-styles and have proposed (in spite of their increasing militancy of attitude, which is largely a reaction to violence done to them by the powers that be) hundreds of programs for a beautiful and humane world society. The growth of the activities of the counterculture and of its need for an educative and informative voice, one born of its own view of the world, for both its own people and those beyond its community who would understand and sympathize with its goals, constitutes the principal reason for the existence of the underground press.

After Kennedy's death, the forces acting within the counterculture toward the proliferation of the underground press were many: the subcultural vacuum created by the *Götterdämmerung* of the beat generation of the 1950's; increased sexual freedom and openness of sexual attitudes, particularly because of the pill; the birth of a new humane conscience through folk music and folk-rock; the explosive sound of a new kind of rock music, psychedelic and more directly responsive to its audience than the music of the 1950's; the search for alternative modes of consciousness through marijuana, LSD, and so forth; the uprising at Berkeley, which proved the manipulative muscle-power of organized demonstrations; poverty programs and the activities of SNCC, CORE, and SDS in their attempts to politically awaken concerned Americans to injustice and the possibilities for coexistence with the third world. Jacob Brackman sums up the entire spectrum of forces: "Given a new youth, a new bohemia, a new iconoclastic humor, a new sexuality, a new sound, a new turn-on, a new abolitionism, a new left, a new hope and a new cynicism, a new press was inevitable."[10]

The underground press came into existence not simply to proclaim, interpret, and direct the movement of the forces listed above, but also to make known the writers' frustrations. Its voice was clearly one of complaint and dissent, as well as affirmation. Ethel Grodzins Romm, in her informative and well-written book on the underground press, *The Open Conspiracy: What America's Angry Generation Is Saying*, helpfully summarizes the moods prevalent at the beginning of its growth:

> The new journals are published by young people dissatisfied to the point of rebellion with the quality of their American lives. In the beginning, in 1965, '66, '67, they were against the Vietnam war, against Puritanical sex, and for marijuana legalization or, as the button said, "Peace Pussy Pot." They were pinning on another generation's Beatnik slogan. In 1964, before the street-corner press sprouted, Students for a Democratic Society (SDS) was selling campaign buttons reading, "Part of the way with LBJ." "Right after the election," said an SDSer, "after winning that tremendous peace mandate, Johnson opted for Goldwater's Vietnam policy. That turned me off elec-

toral politics forever. In this country we elect a dictator every four years."

For the first time an American president was labeled "illegitimate." His government was no longer thought to be responsive to the will of the people. There could be no loyal opposition. All those savage buttons, "Chicken Little Was Right," "I Am a Human Being—Do Not Fold, Spindle, or Mutilate," "Make Love Not War," "Kill a Commie For Christ," "Smoking Is Safer Than Breathing," "Here Come De Mace," "I Am the Americong"—they were headlines waiting for someone to come along and write the stories. The first newspapers were anti-war, anti-parent, anti-middle class, anti-system.[11]

The journalists lashing out were not always talented writers, but their message was as clear as those of the buttons, both as dissent and as a plea for political sanity and existential wholeness.

The first significant voice of the new underground of the 1960's was the Los Angeles *Free Press*, founded in 1964 by its editor-publisher Art Kunkin, a former machinist, free-lance photographer, and student of Manhattan's New School for Social Research. The paper was modeled after the *Village Voice* and was described in 1966 by Kunkin as "a forum for free expression of critical comment and dialogue."[12] The weekly *Free Press* (or *Freep*, as it's called) began as a free eight-page, 5,000-edition tabloid and grew to sixteen pages and a circulation of 9,000 by 1966. In 1968 it was the most successful and professional underground paper, slightly more leftist than the *Voice*, with a circulation of 68,000, a staff of thirty-two, and a gross annual income of $450,000. It has grown since 1968 to a circulation near 100,000, and success has not ruined it. On the contrary, its success is a tribute to the conscientiousness of the staff and an indication of growth in the underground audience that wants to be informed by its few-holds-barred journalism. Also, unlike many underground papers, the *Free Press* has had an effective and profitable program of classified advertising, from buying and selling to cryptic messages. Its cartoons have been among the best in the underground, particularly the work of Ron Cobb (for instance, a wind-up marine bayonetting a child), and they have been distributed to other papers.

From its inception the *Free Press* helped to define the breadth of underground interests and the journalistic style for communicating those interests. Although it was a paper closely involved with local issues, it broadened from the local coverage characteristic of the *Village Voice* and concerned itself with issues on a national scale: drug busts in Texas, Jim Garrison's Kennedy assassination theories, rock-music, Vietnam, or sexual freedom and be-in's in San Francisco. As much as possible, its reporters were present and involved in the events they wrote about. They sought inside information rather than relying on hearsay or established press releases, and their journalism attempted to communicate factual material as well as a personal style of concern and participation. They had no pretensions to a so-called "objectivity"; for the most part they wrote about what they felt and witnessed. Following the lead of Krassner's *Realist*, they acknowledged no sacred cows.

During the 1950's, imitating and diverging from the *Village Voice*, numerous smaller mimeographed papers were published (for example, *Beatitude* from San Francisco or, from Toronto, *Combustion*) which added to the growing but as yet limited alternative press of dissent. Likewise, after 1964, underground journalism grew rapidly, with many papers following the format and preoccupations of the Los Angeles *Free Press*. Few of those mimeo sheets of the 1950's survived into the 1960's, and the ones that did never reached a large audience, partly because of their heavy leaning toward fetishistic, homosexual, and scatological sexual interests, bad poetry, and off-color or sensationalist politics. However, the papers published after the *Free Press* have had a much better record of survival. They had a growing audience, nationwide and eager for a new journalistic medium; and they were able to assemble staffs of politically dedicated writers and reporters who were conscientious and concerned to reach their audience meaningfully.

Furthermore, a small, local, and unsubsidized paper did not have to depend on the informality, shoddiness, and graphic limitations of the mimeograph, because the new process of cold-type offset printing was available to them. According to Ethel Romm,

This is the printing method that has made possible the entire street-corner press of the 1960's—a cheap, fast, flexible process, only recently used by daily newspapers. The first cold-type offset plant in the world for a daily newspaper was installed in Middletown, New York, in 1956. As it drew visitors from all over the world, the attention was focused on the offset press with its magazine-quality reproductions of photographs on cheap newsprint. But the innovative possibilities for the protest press lie in the "cold-type." No more are long-apprenticed Linotypists required to set column in rigid strips. Now anybody who can hunt and peck can type out the page. Or write it out in long-hand. Or paste pictures on it. Or play Picasso and glue together collages and montages. The camera does not care, it is not a mold for hot metal. It takes one picture of everything which quickly becomes a plate for the offset press. Once the young journalists found they could use offset for less money than mimeograph after about 2,000 copies, they were on their way.[13]

The underground papers, especially those with large local circulations, such as the *East Village Other (EVO)*, the *Seed* from Chicago, the *Avatar* from Boston, and the San Francisco *Oracle*, were quick to explore and experiment with the illustrative and artistic potential of offset reproduction. So, not only did the new process make the papers materially possible, it also allowed the best ones to create a fantastic new style of graphic journalism. The *Oracle*, particularly, has been responsible for making newspaper graphics an art-form, and it published some of the most beautiful and trend-setting psychedelic art of the 1960's.

With a new audience, who wanted to read papers that covered their own scene and bridged the credibility gap in news reporting, many talented writers, and a new method of printing text and designs, the underground proliferated rapidly, and in 1966 two tangible events served to maintain that proliferation: the Supreme Court rulings concerning hard-core pornography and the "redeeming social value" of other forms, which made possible a legal liberalization of sexual candor in the press (to some extent at least: many presses are still harassed by local officials and some have folded from a district attorney making his reputation fighting "obscenity"[14]); and the formation of the Underground Press Syndicate, initiated by Allan and Don Katzman of the *East Village Other*. Of the two events, the second is undoubtedly the more important, for it made possible a distribution and standardization of underground journalism not before possible. There were five original member papers that agreed to exchange, by a one-time reprint right, articles, columns, and cartoons, and to hire a central advertising agency and divide the profit: Manhattan's *East Village Other,* which initiated the syndicate; the Los Angeles *Free Press*; the Berkeley *Barb* from Berkeley, California; the *Paper* from East Lansing, Michigan; and Detroit's *Fifth Estate,* whose title announces the social-political ontology of the underground press.

The brochure of UPS makes clear that the organization's short tradition is one of opposition to the established media and the society they represent and of affirmation of its own audience's ideologies:

> "The Underground Press Syndicate . . . papers are a primary reaction to the plastic computerized society. . . . America has been following ancient myths, the establishment press has propagated them. The sterile old mythology is no longer relevant. The Underground Press is creating a new mythology, more immediate, more relevant. It transcends the 'blue laws of conformity' and reaches out to a new consciousness."[15]

This credo is a condensation of the psychedelic, sexual, and political character of the papers, which were to a great extent extensions of their editors' personalities and beliefs.

Allan Katzman, editor of the *East Village Other,* which was founded by Walter Bowart and John Wilcock and was at the time of the syndicate merger less than a year old with a circulation around 10,000, said of his paper that "We are in favor of evolution, not revolution," something few underground editors would say today, and that "We hope to transform the middle class by internal and external stimuli, by means of media and LSD."[16] *EVO* from the beginning was an avant-garde paper, even among its peers. It was less local than the *Voice* or the Los Angeles *Free Press* and was devoted to the *outré* in an international context, having transcended Zen Buddhism and realpolitik for astrology, macrobiotics, the occult, and advocation of withdrawal from the American scene; and it was in contact with underground culture in England,

Japan, India, and other countries. John Wilcock, previously one of the founding staff-members of the now middle-aged *Voice*, considered *EVO* an artistic, exploratory medium of communication: " 'We're creative artists. . . . We represent our milieu, people pushing the boundaries—and exploring beyond them. We're not interested in shocking anyone, just in reaching the guys who don't think automatically, who feel like us, dig us. We give them a forum and ammunition.' "[17] The paper had a sure audience, and its journalism was as affirmative as it was dissenting in tone. It still constitutes a major voice of the underground.

The Berkeley *Barb*, begun in 1965, the *Free Press's* syndicate brother on the West Coast, was founded and edited by Max Scherr. It was at first primarily a minority "cause" paper and was less sociological than the *Free Press*. The *Barb* was more concerned with immediate political problems than the almost visionary *EVO*, although given somewhat to a journalism of pastoral sexuality. The political foci of the *Barb* were such issues as Vietnam, about which it was radically vocal, and the Chicano grape-pickers strike in Southern California. Scherr tried to keep the paper's field of concerns broad and international, and very largely succeeded, but his New Leftist rhetoric and his diffuse journalistic interests and preachments weakened the paper's voice. Nonetheless, the paper improved and commanded a growing audience, its circulation reaching 90,000 in the summer of 1969 when a squabble arose concerning the financing of the *Barb* staff and operations. The result of the wage-demands and arguing that followed was a revolt of part of the staff, who began to publish their own paper, the *Tribe*.

Nonetheless, the *Barb* continues to be published and, besides having developed in political acumen, offers its audience a column, "Dear Doctor Hip Pocrates," also distributed through the syndicate, that has become an underground classic. The column, written by Dr. Eugene Schoenfeld, an M. D., who was at the University of California Health Center in Berkeley, now at the San Francisco Center for Special Problems, has been a gold mine of humorous and candidly helpful advice about sexual and emotional problems. His writing is the underground's answer to the kind of columns of inane problems and trumped-up advice that one finds in the established press; and many of the best columns have now been assembled in a Grove Press book, *Dear Doctor Hip Pocrates: Advice Your Family Doctor Never Gave You* (New York, 1968).

The *Paper* and the *Fifth Estate* were less significant voices with low circulations, 3,000 and 1,000 respectively. The *Paper*, founded and edited by Michael Kindman, who was a student majoring in history at Michigan State, was principally a stick for beating the bureaucracy at his university (which in 1966 was deeply involved in CIA Vietnam projects) and elsewhere; and Kindman rallied considerable support (several large campus protests) when the administration at Michigan State attempted to suppress his paper, thus setting an important landmark in the defense of journalistic freedom of speech. The *Fifth Estate* was founded and edited by Harvey Ovshinsky, who had worked briefly for the *Free Press*. The *Fifth Estate*, like the *Paper*, has grown and improved somewhat since the syndicate merger, but it also was originally very unprofessional and, perhaps because of Ovshinsky's previous work with the *Free Press*, very derivative; and certainly his paper, consisting mainly of UPS material and mediocre local writing for "the liberals, the hippies and the anarchists," was, like the *Paper*, more dependent on the other members of the syndicate than those members were on it—but then, that is the purpose of a syndicate.

The Underground Press Syndicate slowly grew in strength and efficiency, and it was joined by dozens of other papers, such as the *Great Speckled Bird* of Atlanta, the *North Carolina Anvil* of Durham (which is about as moderate and as acceptable to the local Lions Club as the underground press can be), and the *Seed* of Chicago. Syndicate membership is now slightly over a hundred, including associates and Canadian papers, and has a total audience of well over a million people. The UPS is a central organ of unity, not only for presses interconnected by teletype, telex, and telephoto service, and a national fund of advertising money, but also for the nationwide counterculture which it informs and serves. Its operations are expanding, and it attempts to recruit not only other underground papers but also college and high-school papers, among which there are increasingly radical journalistic voices.

The demand for the syndicate's kind of journalism is growing, and its directors envision a tremendous expansion of activities. In 1967, for example, John Wilcock foresaw "a network of short-range pirate radio stations, outside FCC jurisdiction—a sort of Radio Free America—broadcasting underground to the fettered, yearning masses. Katzman dreams of a giant Consumer's Union paper, which would undermine the dichotomy between employers and workers, uniting all consumerhood, a living entity independent of state and producers."[18]

Granting the short span of time since then, and the complications chaining all experiments and idealisms, much of this dream is on the way to realization; for dozens of underground radio stations are surviving and broadcasting throughout the country, and the underground press continues to publish consumer information and news of food conspiracies to help readers avoid exploitation by the huge American marketing system.

There is, however, another chapter in the history of underground press syndication that must be told, and it concerns Raymond Mungo and the founding of Liberation News Service (LNS), which now boasts a readership of five million. Mungo's book *Famous Long Ago,* the most beautifully personal and informative book available about the underground and its people, tells the story, according to the subtitle, of *My Life and Hard Times with Liberation News Service.* Mungo, Marshall Bloom, and several friends, after running and attempting to radicalize the United States Student Press Association, an activity they quickly abandoned as hopeless, in 1967 formed a competing news service, one which they hoped would promote a freer style of journalism and avoid what was regarded by many presses as the corruption and disorganization of UPS. The Liberation News Service was conceived just before the march on the Pentagon on October 21, 1967. In a meeting of the sanhedrin of the hip (including underground film-makers, Walter Bowart of *EVO* and UPS, and editor Allen Cohen of the San Francisco *Oracle,* as well as a reporter from the Washington *Post*) the goals of LNS were proposed, and the fury of confusion and cross-purposes that arose left little promise for its future. But LNS succeeded two weeks later in sending out stories and photographs of the Pentagon demonstration which were published in part or whole by over a hundred papers and read by over a million people. At that time there were about 250 underground papers in the United States—less than the number which presently receives LNS's $15.00, semiweekly news packet.

The history of LNS was stormy, and Mungo and his friends eventually, after a brutal quarrel, abandoned the organization to the more aggressive and less gentle members of the staff and founded a communal farm in Vermont.[19] LNS is now a member of UPS; claims over 300 subscribers (including over 100 college newspapers); and has become much more militantly radical than it was under Mungo and more committed to New Leftist propagandizing for revolution. Regardless of its subsequent history and its future, LNS was controlled originally by Mungo's enlightened gentleness and a commitment to a new kind of journalism. In *Famous Long Ago* he tells, in his own inimitable style, the story of the organization's beliefs and activities during earlier and more halcyon days:

> We were not sticklers for accuracy—neither is the underground press in general, so *be advised*—but our factual errors were not the product of any conspiracy to mislead the young, but of our own lack of organization, shorthandedness, and impatience with grueling research efforts. *Facts* are less important than *truth* and the two are far from equivalent, you see; for cold facts are nearly always boring and may even distort the truth, but Truth is the highest achievement of human expression. Hmmm. I had better clarify this with an example: let's suppose, for want of better employment, we are watching Walter Cronkite on TV. Uncle Walter, who is cute and lovable and whom we all love, calmly asserts that the Allied Command (!) reports 112 American soldiers were killed in the past week in Vietnam, 236 South Vietnamese died in the same period, and Enemy (*not* Vietnamese?) deaths were "put at" 3,463. Now, I doubt the *accuracy* of that report, but I know it doesn't even come *close* to the *truth*; in fact it is an obscene, inexcusable Lie. Now let's pick up a 1967 copy of Boston *Avatar,* and under the headline "Report from Vietnam, by Alexander Sorensen" read a painfully graphic account of Sorensen's encounter with medieval torture in a Vietnamese village. Later, because we know Brian Keating, who wrote the piece, we discover that Alexander Sorensen doesn't exist and the incident described in *Avatar,* which moved thousands, never in fact happened.

But because it has happened in man's history, and because we know we are responsible for its happening today, and because the story is unvarnished and plain and human, we know it is true, truer than any facts you may have picked up in the *New Republic*. And the same kind of examples could be given for many stories unrelated to the war in Vietnam, all the way down to the dog-bites-man clippings at the bottom of page 38 in today's *Newark Times*. I'm not saying it would be ethical to broadcast a false rumor that all bridges and tunnels leading out of Manhattan are indefinitely closed (though that might be interesting); but I'm saying that the distinctly Western insistence on *facts* (and passive faith in science and technology) betrays our tragically, perhaps fatally, *limited* consciousness of life. The facts, even if he can get them, will never help a man realize who and what he is or aspire to fulfill his natural role in the universe. Ain't it the truth? All we say: tell the truth, brothers, and let the facts fall where they may. . . . They ["most straight journalists"] will write serious accounts of the Chamber of Commerce dinner, the President's press conference, the Thanksgiving football game, millions of facts without even one simple truthful picture of the slavery of Everyman in "this dog-eat-dog world" they inhabit.

LNS and the underground press, in those days at least, tried to tell the world the truth as we saw it. The world is getting up in the morning around 2:00 P.M. Discovering opium. Having sex with somebody you just met. And your best friend. Longing for just an inch of honest black soil under your toes where you could raise one honest cucumber. Begging dimes at the airport (leave the bus station for the old drunks, respect their turf). Arranging the abortion of a child you're not sure you fathered. Bouncing checks. Getting stoned and meeting Christ. Getting busted for getting stoned and meeting Christ. Worrying about tomorrow and the day after tomorrow. Splitting to Morocco. Getting all sick and strung out on Demerol. Tiring of your scene and leaving it. Trusting to God. Trying to be harmless and have fun. Tripping. Looking for a little sense, peace, or justice among powerful men and generally failing to find them. Looking to score.

Playing music everywhere you go. Eating whatever you can get. And writing about everything that happens to you just as it happened.[20]

Mungo is a good writer, and his writing is representative of the best styles to be found in New Journalism, in the underground press or elsewhere. His quest for truth rather than simple facts (whatever the limitations of that idea), the attempt to speak for a new generation of people, and the commitment to an ideal of personal, empirical, morally minded, and creative reportage and commentary—all are the emblems of the best underground press writing and of much of the New Journalism.

2

THE EXPANSION OF
THE
UNDERGROUND PRESS

We have simply got to create anti-
environments in order to know what we are
and what we are doing.

Marshall McLuhan in
*War and Peace in the
Global Village*

People don't need to read about old happenings, dead news, that other newspapers and
televisions and sidewalks are full of. They
don't even want it. There's just nothing
else. I want to give them something. I don't
know what, but I'm trying.

David
in the Boston *Avatar*

There are four other categories of newspaper publications
that are related to the underground press activities I have been
discussing: the Movement or New Left papers, the Black
underground, other special-interest underground papers, and
the high-school underground. The concerns, motivations, and
journalistic styles of all these publications are related, and they
are, in many ways, part of a total publishing community with
the larger underground. However, the separate categories can
be defined, and some comparisons and discussion will be helpful in demonstrating the diversity of the underground as part
of the New Journalism.

Ethel Romm summarizes some of the important distinctions to be made in comparing Movement and underground
papers:

To make some generalizations that do not always apply, a Movement or New Left paper covers "the struggle" for a "new society" soberly. It differs from a street-corner [i.e., "underground"] paper when it does not cover new record releases or rock concerts; does not publish obscenities stridently; rarely experiments with flamboyant layout or typography; prints no pornography; has no essays on oriental philosophies or astrology; accepts no sex ads; is not evangelical about drugs; is not hawked on the streets or distributed through regular newsstands. . . . Street-corner papers, unlike the subsidized Movement papers, must survive in the capitalistic system they decry. . . . Established newspapers work for reform; street-corner and Movement papers, if they are not for revolution, share an abiding bitterness about the State of the Union.[1]

Movement papers are more analytical and more tightly focused on the Leftist political position they affirm. Strictly speaking, their style of journalistic writing is frequently more traditional than that of the true underground, and in that sense they are not clearly a part of the New Journalism; but their programmatic maintenance of a journalistic practice that is radically opposed to the established press ideologically qualifies them, in a broader sense, as illustrative of the New Journalism.

The most well-known of the national Movement papers are the *Movement, SDS New Left Notes,* and the *Guardian.* The *Movement,* which is now unaffiliated, was originally the publication of the Student Nonviolent Coordinating Committee (which now has its own *SNCC Newsletter*) and is now an important organ in the promotion of radical organizations and community political-social projects, somewhat in the fashion of labor-organization newspapers in the 1930's, although the comparison won't hold very far. *SDS New Left Notes* is the paper of Students for a Democratic Society and publishes for its several thousand members nationwide. It has been a sometimes effective, sometimes confused platform for the communication of student activities and realpolitik and has, like the established press (though in a different way), promoted such New Leftist ideologues and activists as Mark Rudd and Staughton Lynd to the center of the national stage of political controversy. The *Guardian,* the oldest of these papers, was founded in 1948 in support of Henry Wallace's candidacy for president. It is a very professional paper and attempts to be traditionally journalistic and objective in its news coverage, more so than any other Movement paper. The *Guardian* is now a cooperatively owned weekly with a circulation exceeding 30,000, and like most underground and Movement papers, it has become increasingly more revolutionary and militant during the last few years.

One of the *Guardian's* more stringent voices is that of Julius Lester, the poet–columnist–folk-singer revolutionary, who contributes a column toward the paper's function of reporting, analyzing and relating to "the world-wide movement against imperialism, wherever it may be found."[2] He is very much aware of the importance of dissenting media, particularly the underground and Movement newspapers:

> The American press is not free, because it accepts the ideology of the government and the system. It does not editorialize against capitalism, imperialism, or free enterprise. It does not question the status quo; it merely suggests various means whereby the status quo may prevail. Thus, we have, in effect, a government-controlled press, because that press is not opposed to the government, but merely to the way the government does what it does.
>
> Because it is a government-controlled press, its reportage of protest and resistance activities, organizations, etc., reflects this bias. It reports events in such a manner that the reportage becomes a weapon to stifle anti-government activity and a weapon to rally government support. This modus operandi can be called "negative news."
>
> Example: In the early decades of this century, whites attacked and killed blacks on numerous occasions. These were reported as "race riots," though it was the whites who were armed and it was blacks who died. What would have been the effect if they had been reported as "massacres," which in fact they were. . . .
>
> The only relationship the press can have to any radical or revolutionary organization is negative, to be used as tools for the government. . . . It is not the function of the press to report; its function is to shape opinion.
>
> It therefore becomes necessary for the left to develop its own means of communication. These can stem from leaflets to newspapers. The Underground Press is a

good development, as are newspapers such as the *Movement*, the *SNCC Newsletter*, *Muhammad Speaks*, the *Guardian*, and others.[3]

The Movement and underground presses *have* elaborated new means of communication and a new rhetoric for articulating and shaping the opinions of the left.

The example of established-press rhetoric that Lester points out is especially important, because it, along with other examples he gives, illustrates the kind of distorted, irrelevant, or null reportage black Americans have received from that press. To borrow an example from Brackman, when the San Francisco *Examiner* speaks of the "civil rights situation" in Oakland, California, and the Berkeley *Barb* speaks of "brutality and segregation in Oakland," one has a sense of the political and rhetorical polarities involved. Many of the underground papers, like the *Barb*, have been openly and committedly sympathetic to the black cause for justice and civil rights, although that sympathy has not had a really strong and central emphasis in a lot of the underground newspapers, whose journalism is more diffuse. Certainly, in this respect, the *Barb* and the *Free Press* have been pioneers, but Movement and New Left papers have been more serious and continuous in their commitment to black politics than have many of the underground papers.[4]

However, with the emergence of black nationalism in its various forms came the need for a black press, a loud and articulate voice that would go far beyond the *Ebony*-magazine brand of black journalism and come directly from the black people themselves, rather than from a predominantly white, if concerned, underground.[5] *Muhammad Speaks*, the Black Muslim paper of the early and mid-1960's, proposed a new set of black-nationalist cultural possibilities and offered a new kind of political-religious identity for black people, but its kind of journalism has given way to more militant and revolutionary voices in such papers as the *Black Panther*, published from Panther headquarters in Oakland, California, since the spring of 1967 when it was founded by Bobby Seale, Huey Newton, and Eldridge Cleaver. Publication of the *Panther* was really a survival necessity, when one considers the biased coverage the Oakland *Tribune* had been giving Panther activities. The Panthers had to make their own side of events known and to expose what they considered to be police harassment, which harassment has since pushed their organization toward an aggressive militancy it did not have in the beginning.

Although there are still some less radical voices in the black underground, such as the very nearly overground *Amistad: Writings on Black History and Culture,* edited by John A. Williams and Charles F. Harris, a journal with a literary bias that recently published its first issue, the dominant and defensive bias has been toward a hard-left, militant kind of journalism with its own set of racial prejudices. Much of this journalism is reaching into and influencing the large underground press, and its papers frequently carry articles concerning or by black leaders such as Eldridge Cleaver or Bobby Seale, whose writing is forceful, persuasive, and intelligent. Underground papers frequently have special issues devoted to some black situation, ghetto problems, or police harassment. Nonetheless, an independent black press is slowly growing, with dozens of papers, usually eight pages or so, with small, local circulations. Most of them are militant enough and their commentary on local problems pointed enough that they experience a good deal of conflict with district attorneys, university administrations, and so forth; and for that reason, or because of financing problems, lack of support, or other limitations, they don't publish for very long.

There are many special-interest underground papers. All of the underground presses are in a sense special-interest presses, and certainly they all, one way or another, represent a minority voice; but there are other group- or problem-specific voices that may be discerned. Special-interest papers spring up constantly in many places, with varied concerns; some last awhile, riding a particular fad of concern to its exhaustion, and some endure with the interest they represent. It would be impossible to mention all of them, but there are several that share part of the ideologies and audience of the larger underground. For instance, *El Malcriado,* a Chicano (Mexican-American) newspaper published in Delano, California, grew up with the grape-pickers strike, an issue which has been widely publicized by UPS and LNS papers. It is not only a "cause" paper in the fullest sense, but is also a voice of identity for an oppressed and, until recently, unheard minority whose problems command strong sympathy from the New Left and underground counterculture. It is one of many small papers arising to the cause of brown power.

Likewise, there are a few American Indian papers that are "cause" papers, speaking for a minority and reifying its identity, pleading for justice, demanding red power, and exposing the ineptitudes and immoralities in the mainstream of American culture and politics. *Akwesasne Notes,* a monthly newspaper published by the Indian Studies Program at Wesleyan University in Middletown, Connecticut, is an example. The paper's editorial office is on the Akwesasne Mohawk Reservation in Hogansburg, New York, and it is controlled and most of it written by Indians. It makes use of both established and underground press news, drawing reportage from the Los Angeles *Free Press,* as well as the Washington *Post* or the San Francisco *Chronicle;* and, of course, the larger underground (as well as the established press, in its own fashion) has devoted considerable writing to the Indians, the San Francisco *Oracle* leading the way during 1967 with an extravagant cultism of the Indian, who is associated with hip culture's pastoral sense of values and who is a living reminder of America's rape of its own natural landscape, belief in technology rather than humanity, and oppression of its own people.

Besides the racially oriented underground, there are, as examples of other special interests, ecologically and pastorally oriented papers, like the *Green Revolution* and *Earth Times,* which are more underground in style than, for instance, *Environment,* a journal published by the Committee for Environmental Information in St. Louis, which is concerned with the particular problem of the effect of technology on the environment. The *Green Revolution,* published monthly by the School of Living in Freeland, Maryland, is devoted to "A world-wide effort for decentralization and rural revival." It is concerned with returning to rural and communal life-styles, and features writing by such people as Hugh Romney (also called "Wavey Gravy"), head of the Hog Farm, the most famous traveling commune since Ken Kesey and his Merry Pranksters made a psychedelic odyssey around the United States in the mid-1960's. The paper is also concerned with alternative and more pastoral kinds of education and the free-culture, Theobaldian economic ideas of the California Diggers and their seventeenth-century counterparts. Broadly speaking, the *Green Revolution,* which was actually begun in the 1940's, represents an attempt to communicate values that will transform the fallacious ecological and social consciousness of its readers toward a sense of natural, rather than technological, living, an effort wholly attuned to the teleology of the larger underground.

The *Earth Times* suggests by the title its differences from, say, the New York *Times*: its values and rhetoric are pastoral, not urban, and natural, not technocratic. The paper, published in San Francisco, rejects the world-view of what it calls the Flat Earth Society (those complacent enough to believe that we live, in effect, on a terrestrial plane which is infinite and therefore possessed of an infinitely exploitable environment) and affirms the Round Earth Society (that enlightened and dedicated, hopefully growing minority who realize that we live on Buckminster Fuller's "spaceship earth," that our environment is limited, and that the biosphere must be preserved before we perish). In general, it reports on activities related to the ecological crisis. It is more professionally a "cause" paper than the *Green Revolution* and is less underground in terms of journalistic style, format, and audience. Although its concerns are shared by most of the underground, it is ideologically closer to the Sierra Club than Romney's Hog Farm.

Most of the underground papers carry reviews and articles on rock music, but there are also a number of papers devoted specifically to the music and its culture—which means a good part of the counterculture in general. The best to date are the *Rolling Stone* and *Crawdaddy*. The *Rolling Stone*, published in San Francisco and edited by Jann Wenner, who was previously rock critic for the *Daily Californian* at Berkeley, is more strictly a rock paper than *Crawdaddy* and has been the vehicle of some of the finest rock criticism of the 1960's. It is an informative paper; its coverage is world-wide; and its music reviews are reliable and intelligent. Although, like *Crawdaddy*, it concerns itself to some extent with nonmusical activities (like the Chicago trial) or other art forms (it features movie reviews), it places its primary journalistic stress on the music and the musicians; and its interviews with rock musicians are probably the best done and most thorough to be found in any of the rock papers. *Crawdaddy*, published in New York, was previously edited by Chester Anderson, a very capable rock journalist, now by Peter Stafford. Under Anderson's editorship it was a magazine; under Stafford it has the format of a newspaper. Its rock journalism is now comparable to that of *Rolling*

Stone, though generally not quite so consistently good; and its concerns tend to be broader, as I said above. It offers movie reviews and some political news, as does *Rolling Stone,* but it also features articles on astrology, futuristic speculations about man's religiopsychological evolution, more poetry than *Rolling Stone,* and more articles concerned with drug culture, as well as some excellent journalistic portraits of rock musicians and analyses of their music.

A GI underground press has proliferated within the army's ranks during the last years, while opposition to the Vietnam war, to the military-industrial complex, and to personal oppression has grown within American society at large. The growth of the GI press (which now publishes several dozen papers, most of them mimeographs printed at bases across the country), like that of the so-called "coffeehouse movement," is probably due in large part to the number of politically aware young men who have been drafted into the army. The GI papers are a voice which the soldier has never had before. They report with candor and conscience that large numbers of soldiers refuse to go to Vietnam or that they participate in peace marches, and the papers have become important as means of expressing outrage concerning the treatment of military prisoners in prisons such as the Presidio in California. The growth of the GI press is a sign of its significance and necessity as a medium for conveying the truth about a minority culture, the dissenting soldier, and is an indication of the power of the impulse to create an underground press that opposes the arbitrary authority and corrupt political structure of a system that remains relatively unexamined by the established press.

There are other kinds of underground press publications which may be pointing the way toward future developments, such as comic books ("comix") like *Zap, Snatch,* and *Big Ass,* or comic papers like the *Gothic Blimp Works* published by *EVO.* (A fascinating article on the comix is Jacob Brackman's "The International Comix Conspiracy," *Playboy,* December 1970, pp. 195 ff.) But perhaps the most significant kind of publication is the pornographic or erotic papers, frequently affiliated with or published by the larger urban underground papers, particularly those in New York City, such as *Kiss* and *Pleasure* (both by part of the *EVO* staff), *Screw* (by part of the

Rat staff), and the New York *Review of Sex* (by part of the now defunct New York *Free Press* staff). Most of these papers are significantly different from typical nudie magazines and *Police Gazette*-type publications. They see their function, as do intelligent nudist magazines like *Ankh,* as the liberation of their audience from the sexual repression traditional in American society. Unlike magazines such as *Playboy* or *Penthouse,* they are committed to paying more than lip service to radical and healthy sexual ideologies and frequently lend informative support to movements like Women's Liberation. They are partly an outgrowth of the personal columns featured in the back pages of many underground papers and, like those columns, cater to a varied audience of the curious and the concerned, swingers, freaks, and alienated individuals—but usually with an enlightened sense of responsibility; and after all, the alienated find solace in *Life* and *Reader's Digest* also. Clearly there is a widespread readiness to accept such papers, because they enjoy large circulations; and the best of them, such as *Screw,* which is usually pictorially interesting, verbally articulate, and humorous, serve an important role as educational and entertaining journalism.

The high-school underground has evolved more recently than the larger underground, which published some writing from high-school students before they began to form their own presses and is still interested in their writing and publishing, as a kind of older brother. According to Diane Divoky, a writer on education and editor of *How Old Will You Be in 1984?,* a collection of *Expressions of Student Outrage from the High School Free Press,* two tenets underlie the journalism of the high-school underground:

> both are reactions to the most characteristic aspects of the culture today. One is that, in this depersonalized, technological society, what is most needed is feeling. The emotional content of an idea, an experience, a commitment is what gives it value, what can be trusted. The adult is told: "You don't understand." Often this means: "You don't feel anything about this. It's just an intellectual exercise for you." Gut reactions, awareness, vibrations are the surest signs of reality in a world where rhetoric is phony, and "reason" and "common sense" become the weapons of the defenders of the status quo.

This passion goes hand-in-hand with a puritanical
zeal for a rigorous ethic, an insistence on absolute honesty
in public and private life. The students are uncompro-
mising and see diplomacy as duplicity, ambivalence as
weakness, and strategic maneuvering as a cop-out.[6]

This double theme of feeling and honesty runs through all the
papers of the underground, not only those of the high schools,
and is basic not only to the style of their journalism (and to the
style of most of the New Journalism), but to the life-style of
their writers and audience as well.

That theme is part of the ideology that defines the counterculture and is slowly but powerfully transforming the political
and personal lives of high-school students. High-school administrators are deluded and paranoiac most of the time when
they search for "outside" influences on this transformation, for
the students running the presses and their audience are themselves deeply aware of the problems of American culture, of
the kinds of oppression and harassment they experience in their
own schools, and of the activities of the hip and radical cultures in their society; and that awareness has been brought
about partly by the established media but more largely by the
students' own desire to learn the truth, to live by feeling and
honesty.

The energy and commitment of high-school students who
have grown beyond the Eagle-Scout Father-Knows-Best arche-
types of the middle of this century have made possible, according to Divoky's estimate, nearly 500 dissenting papers, most of
which do not last very long, usually because of the pressure of
an administration that feels threatened and (usually is and
should be) questioned—and usually the pressure itself becomes
a central journalistic topic until the paper dies. Like the true
underground papers, those of the high schools are not only
dissenting but, as Divoky pointed out, also searching for new
life-styles and proposing possibilities for the rehumanization of
their schools and society. While putting down their school's
incredibly irrelevant dress codes and rigorously unjust tracking
systems, they also elevate the love-freedom ethos of the most
knowledgeable and historically precarious generation that has
ever existed; and the journalistic language of both efforts can
range from being careful and objective to being surrealistic
and what their administrators would regard as obscene, but it

is always personal, frequently *ad hominem,* honest, and born of feeling.

Certainly the high-school underground does not represent or speak to all high-school students, any more than *EVO* does all the people of New York City; but it is important and growing, and it represents a movement on the part of many students toward a kind of radical and meaningful education that most high schools don't promote. Their intelligence in implementing that journalistic education is amazing, when one considers the programmed and provincial mentality of almost all high-school students only half a decade ago. Furthermore, somewhat after the example of UPS, many of the papers have gone together to form the High School Independent Press Service (HIPS) of New York City, a news bureau which distributes items mainly to other high-school papers in New York, where, incidentally, most of the high-school free-press activity is occurring. Jon Grell of HIPS is very much aware of the educational function of the high-school papers and of the underground press as a tool of communication. Speaking of the community of the underground press, he says

> We are a group of people who offer an alternative life style to that of the establishment. The word "alternative" is extremely important. We offer a completely viable way of living which concerns the socio-economic-political aspects of society; a new society, hopefully one which will be better than the present financially oriented society. . . .
>
> These papers [of the larger underground] accomplished the politicizing of the people who were just turning on to the "New Politics." Today, when papers like *The New York Times* are able to control the minds and actions of its readers in the way that it deems necessary for the "good" of society, it can quiet the news in such a way that the people don't even know what's happening. Take for instance, the whole Vietnam war issue. It was played down in the press of this country prior to 1964 so that a vast majority of Americans didn't even know where Vietnam was. It was the underground press that made as many people as possible aware of what was going on. Take also the actions on the Columbia campus last spring. Who knew more about what truly happened: the readers of *The New York Times* or the readers of the *Rat?* The

underground press deals in education, not in the stifling of issues.

This is also the case in high schools throughout the country. It is even more accentuated in the high schools because the ages of people attending high schools allows [sic] their minds to be more malleable, even though they may be totally apathetic or staunch "Wallace supporters." These people must be educated, and an underground paper is the only way of reaching an entire student body. An article about white racism in high schools will get more people talking and thinking than an article about the latest basketball game in the administration-sanctioned paper.[7]

Grell's statement is closely parallel to what most underground editors would say, in high schools and elsewhere, and he points out an important secondary educational function of the underground press: the actual audience of an underground paper, as of any paper—perhaps this holds more so for one of the underground—is not simply its readers, who frequently read a paper passed around three or four times from the original buyer (something that seldom happens with most newspapers), but also the people who discuss issues and ideas with underground readers. As an example of the audience-commanding power of the underground, here the high-school underground, is the *New York High School Free Press*'s proud report that John Lindsay named their paper as one of the "six major reasons for student unrest" in New York City[8]—a heavy accusation against a "high-school" newspaper. There are several dozen other papers in high schools across the country that are just as articulate, if not yet that powerful, like the *American Revelation* from Elgin, Illinois, the *Open Door* from Milwaukee, and the *South Hampton Illustrated Times* from Detroit. The developing writers of the New Journalism are legion. Just as many of the creative journalists on college campuses have gone over to the large underground, so many of those in high school have given up reporting on the school dance in favor of educating and being educated through their own free press.

The underground press may also be thought of as including some "little magazines," a form of publication which for years has presented itself as an alternative to established and more traditional journals and magazines, and which is usually more literary, although increasingly sociological and pop-oriented of late, than political. One doesn't think of little magazines in general as being part of the underground, and they are usually more concerned with poetry, fiction, and short essays than with writing that is really journalistic in style; but there are some that began publication within the last few years and, perhaps, a few older ones that have become politicalized or radicalized, whose rhetoric is frequently editorializing in character and/or journalistic in style, and that share the interests and causes of the underground newspapers. In addition, there are some magazines, such as *US* and *Countdown,* which can easily be seen as part of the journalism of the underground press, the latter particularly, since much of its material is from UPS.

In 1967 Jacob Brackman listed three little magazines that he considered significant members of the underground: the media-defying *Fuck You: A Magazine of the Arts* from New York, edited by Ed Sanders, a poet and lead singer of The Fugs, a psychic-frontier-exploring rock group, who declared his magazine dedicated to "pacifism, national defense through nonviolent resistance, unilateral disarmament, multilateral indiscriminate apertural conjugation, anarchism, world federalism, civil disobedience"[9] and so on toward a vision of a sex-hashish paradise under the watchful eye of J. Edgar Hoover (Sanders is a brilliant and flamboyant spokesman for his underground generation, in spite of and because of his wide-ranging, comic, and fleshly intellectualism, and his editorials are marvelous parodies of established media journalism); *Gargoyle,* which promised to publish "what Ed Sanders rejects"; and *Resurgence,* founded in 1964 as the literary voice of the Resurgence Youth Movement which, again quoting from Brackman, is "a new anarchist movement based on the world revolution of youth and the birth of a new psychedelic Afrasian-American soul"[10] and which is characterized by a kind of hysterical, poetic journalism prophesying the apocalypse and urging a total, mystical-sexual-political world revolution.

In addition to those, there are, among others, four little magazines of particular interest that have been issued since Brackman's article was written: *Avant Garde, US, Countdown,* and *Fruitcup. Avant Garde* is the most professionally done of the magazines and in many ways is not a little magazine at all. However, its audience is, I suspect, much the same as that of the underground press; and its political, sexual, and artistic interests are kin to those of the underground papers. Since it began publication from New York in January 1968, editor Ralph Ginzburg has become a martyr-hero for the cause of freedom from censorship and for free speech and open sexual expression—causes close to the heart of the underground. The magazine is beautifully illustrated and features some of the most imaginative and finely printed erotic art being published, such as that of Melle Oldeboerrigter, the modern Dutch counterpart of Hieronymous Bosch. It also publishes poetry, sociological essays, fiction, and *outré* scientific articles—all with a countercultural bias.

US, which began publication in June 1969, made a stronger bid as a new kind of little magazine than did *Avant Garde*. Under the editorship of Richard Goldstein, the pop-journalist and rock-critic, *US* was and still is aimed at the underground audience, and its glossy cover and pop-art format give it the appearance of a complete and "in" document of its time. The mixing of types, the politico-sexual comic strips, the far-out graphics and artwork, the advertisement of "All the News That's Fit to Eat," the collages and the journalistic style—all announce its push toward a new kind of underground-magazine message. *US* is much more concerned with immediate issues than *Avant Garde*, although it does feature poetry and fiction; but the style of its journalistic writing—creative, personal, eclectic—is in the frontier of New Journalism. The magazine attunes itself to the political pop-rock pulse of its readers and attracts some very articulate and experienced writers, journalists and otherwise.

Countdown is associated with both UPS and LNS and, though the magazine has its own able writers, is composed largely of syndicated material. However, that is also the great value of the magazine, because the reader has a chance to read the best writing from a number of papers. Thus, *Countdown* is very much a magazine by and about the underground press, a sort of underground-in-summary published five times a year, starting in February 1970. In the first article of that issue, John Wilcock praised the activities of the underground and suggested that *Countdown* would align itself with those activities:

> The underground press is the loving product of the best minds of my generation. . . . The underground press is

part of the scene, rather than reporting on it, as do conventional papers. . . . The underground press is flexible. . . . The underground press is resilient. . . . The underground press is everywhere. . . .

The underground press is ingenious, too. Faced with a limited budget, in fact, unbelievably limited by any standards (most underground papers have a budget about equal to a NY *Times* copyboy's salary) they have taken newsprint and made it a medium of art and revolution.[11]

Like *US*, perhaps partly in answer to it, *Countdown* also experiments with graphics, photography, and types to illustrate and emphasize its writing, which is almost entirely journalistic.

Fruitcup's issue "No. Zero" was published from New York in 1969, undated as to month but, although it has the appearance of a quick book printed on cheap paper, promising to appear again. The magazine features bizarre, and sometimes clever and imaginative, collages and montages to support its collection of writings from such people as Allen Ginsberg, Abbie Hoffman, Ed Sanders, and a dozen other well-known people on the revolutionary fringe of the future. The predominance of poetry and creative prose writing suggests that it is a typical little magazine, but its pose beyond that is as an underground publication—radical, politically apocalyptic, sexually open.

There are many stories that could be amassed to illustrate the history and diversification of the underground press—for instance, an account of the political conflicts of the Boston *Avatar*, perhaps the most beautifully professional of the underground papers; a discussion of the evolution of the New York *Rat*, an SDS-oriented, strictly political paper which caters to an emerging armed-revolutionary mentality and strongly supports the Women's Liberation movement; or a report on the underground press outside the United States—but the developments which I have outlined and discussed constitute a short but informative sketch of how the underground participates in the New Journalism. I hope that the history has been illustrative and exemplary rather than boringly "thorough," and I hope I have offered a kind of guide to the discovery of the underground. There remains, however, the need to evaluate briefly the change that has occurred in the underground press during the last five years.

In 1967 the San Francisco *Oracle* was a principal organ of the underground and thrived handsomely on hippie-seeking tourists, as well as its more attuned public, during the "Summer of Love" in the Haight-Ashbury district. Sometimes lyrical, sometimes intellectual, sometimes comic or maybe maudlinly serious, it was, as Brackman says, "the gentlest and loveliest of the underground papers," with its Hinduism, pastoralism, astrology, and hopeful love messages for a society of freedom and happiness.[12] It, with the Diggers and their propaganda branch, The Communication Company, was at the center of a communal dream. But with the end of the "Summer of Love," that dream in San Francisco began to dissolve—partly because of the bad drugs being sold, partly because of crime in Haight-Ashbury, police harassment, and general disillusionment. The dissolution was a complex event and perhaps will never be fully understood. Furthermore, the *Oracle* folded at the beginning of autumn because of the departure of most of the hippies and tourists who bought the paper and because of internal difficulties.

The dissolution of the dream and the folding of the *Oracle* were both important events in the history of the counterculture and the underground press. They were symbolic, and to some extent promotive, of the changes that began to occur in the press and its audience. The papers and their culture began to drift away from gentleness toward more bitter political interests, more militant radicalism, and more shock-value sex. This change is not a dreamed-up political act of hundreds of underground editors; it is largely a reaction to the increasing militance of police, university administrators, and the "silent majority" against dissent and the values and life-styles of the counterculture—a militance which culminated in the murdering of students at Kent State in Ohio and at Jackson State in Mississippi.

There are dozens of reasons for establishment and radical militance, such as the indifference of administrative bureaucrats to the voice of the counterculture. The underground and established media are preoccupied with speculations about the conflicts across the generation gap. That is general talk, and it is beyond my purposes here to collect all the evidence for an elaborate etiology of revolutionary attitudes; the point is that the shift toward militance has occurred, and that it is implemented and reflected to some extent by all of the underground papers, though some of them are more militant than others. Perhaps it will deepen their commitment and increase their circulation and relevance; perhaps it will alienate some of their present audience or create a new one; perhaps it will play out its violent revolutionary fervor into something more useful, human, and lasting, or, through the press, escalate into more nationwide disaster and bloodshed. Whether or not one considers the change morally justified, it seems to be driving the papers toward an identity closer to that of the World War II European underground, which may be exciting or even, by some incompetence, necessary, but it is destroying a lot of their beauty as newspapers of the New Journalism. If the established media had been doing their real job all along, there would probably have been no change toward militance and intolerance on either side of the cultural fence—and the lack of need for an underground press would have been a small price to pay.

Though there is still some gentleness and love in the rhetoric of the press, there is a militant disaffection and violence too—and both voices must be heard if one is to be aware of the significance of the underground press and the New Journalism and avoid the fantasy that the world is somehow, in a time of chaos and misunderstanding, operating by "business as usual." Raymond Mungo, since his break with LNS, speaks of the organization as "a monstrous, repressive form of expression, a Frankenstein we had created but later disposed of, something very much in the past and good riddance to it. LNS was one of those things we had left behind when we came over to the New Age."[13] Perhaps, like LNS, it will be the fate of the underground press to lose many of its gentlest and most intelligent writers and readers, as they try to find a means of survival beyond its increasingly confused and fear-compromised world. Perhaps, as Marat says in Peter Weiss' *Marat/ Sade*, the most important act for each individual of the counter-culture, and of the planet Earth, is "to turn yourself inside out/ and see the whole world with fresh eyes" and to communicate the possibilities rather than the liabilities of being human. Then we will have created "a bigger underground press than ever, for each hath one and is one."[14]

3

THREE MAJOR STYLISTS: TRUMAN CAPOTE, TOM WOLFE, AND NORMAN MAILER

> . . . translating the entire world into
> a work of art.
>
> Marshall McLuhan in
> *War and Peace in the
> Global Village*

The underground press has been a steady champion of freedom of speech, no matter how gross or inarticulate that speech might be. Its cause was boosted by the Free Speech Movement at Berkeley in 1964 (a more complex event than the name indicates) and by many other freedoms of dissent exercised since that time. Motivated by a desire to be direct, personal, and imaginative, to "tell it like it is," the press has tried in part, like Wordsworth, to return to the language of the common man. But that language is mixed with hip vernacular, "obscenities," rhetorical flights, poetic *Schwärmerei*, as well as good standard English. It looks frequently like just affected bad grammar, and it is occasionally self-consciously like ghetto jive (though the translation of black slang into hip English has been going on for a long time). Nonetheless, this new language of the press and its culture is coming close to creating a new mainstream of English, and, more importantly for my purpose here, it has been an impetus for, as well as a part of, New Journalistic style.

To gain a simple impression of the writing style of the New Journalists, one may compare an edition of, say, the New York *Times* with one of *EVO*, but the more complex transformations in journalistic style are found in the work of individual writers. Some of these writers have been affiliated with the underground press at some point in their careers, some have not; most of them are writers by profession, but many are not. In one way or another they have abandoned traditional journalistic styles and experimented with new ones, with a new vocabulary, a new voice, a new sense of events that is immediate, personal, close to the pulse of present history.

I think that the principal distinguishing mark of New Journalistic style is the writer's attempt to be personalistic, involved, and creative in relation to the events he reports and comments upon. His journalism, in general, has no pretense of being "objective" and it bears the clear stamp of his commitment and personality. However, this isn't always the case, because some New Journalists have experimented with new techniques of objectivity, rather like *cinéma vérité,* and write with a renewed commitment to factual thoroughness (which frequently endows muckraking, as long as it's true, with a new kind of significance). In general, the style of New Journalism is a response to the radically new kinds of events and personalities that are shaping American and world culture; it is an attempt to record and evaluate history by keeping language and attitude closely attuned and responsive to the style of events.

A clear indication of some of the differences between traditional journalism and New Journalism may be seen by examining a book entitled *The Working Press,* edited by Ruth Adler (Toronto, New York, and London: Bantam Books, 1966). It is a collection of stories "behind the news" by New York *Times* reporters, such as Tom Wicker (on John Kennedy's assassination) and David Halberstam (on the Vietnam war). Each reporter narrates an intriguing, sometimes humorous, sometimes terrifying, account of his own experience and other events that were not reported by the *Times* when it printed the reporter's coverage of a particular situation. The essence of the traditional journalistic esthetic is obvious here: it is dependent on a distilling, depersonalizing, objectifying, and rendering innocuous of official reportage. The New Journalist would be much more interested in writing the "behind the news" report than in producing the watered-down account that is offered a buying public that the paper can't risk offending or psychologically transforming. He would be governed by a sense of how the events he encountered were constellated, how they affected his own feelings and thinking, and how they constituted a concrete human experience for him or other people involved; and he would then make a "journal" of the event, a novelistic or impressionistic reconstruction, or an extended and thorough document.

Recalling Raymond Mungo's distinction between "facts" and "truth" in reporting, one may discern part of the role of the underground press in shaping a New Journalistic style and also notice a significant trait of the established press: it relies upon a curt, distilled reportage that is governed by rhetorical and editorial clichés that are unrelated to the character of events reported. New Journalism, on the other hand, keeps its rhetorical devices flexibly open to events, and its style responds in kind. The so-called "objectivity" or "facts" of the established press are usually "in front of the news." The New Journalist's interest in the stories "behind the news" is really only a starting point for arriving at the *tertium quid,* the central human events implied by the "behind" and the "in front of."

The use of alternative styles is not a new idea entirely, but it has come to a variegated and widespread fruition only in the latter half of the 1960's. John Hersey's *Hiroshima,* published in 1946, was a brilliant *tour de force* in journalistic writing, and it is some credit to *Time* and *Life* that he served as their correspondent during World War II. Having interviewed several survivors immediately after the bombing, Hersey set about writing a sort of novelistic reconstruction of the event as those people experienced it. It is a deeply moving and compassionate account of suffering and small, desperate heroisms; and its technique foreshadows journalistic experiments like Truman Capote's nonfiction novel, *In Cold Blood,* the story of the Clutter family murder, published in 1965. The underground press of the 1950's, such as it was, was undoubtedly influential to some extent in encouraging new styles; and one could return to Upton Sinclair's *The Jungle,* or much of nineteenth-century naturalistic fiction, for examples of the adaptation of a traditional literary genre, the novel, to journalistic or pseudojournalistic writing. Also, the idea of personalistic journalism is not new at all, but it is only recently that it has become really acceptable, significant in quantity, and, particularly, shaped into an esthetically coherent and vitally informative literature. It is difficult to assess New Journalistic styles abstractly; it is better to turn to the stylists themselves to learn how they differ from their predecessors. Perhaps the most important thing to remember is that, for all of these journalists, the radical character of events during the 1960's forced them to find new and more relevant voices for giving reality to human experience.

There is a certain amount of elasticity in my concept of the New Journalism (although I don't think that elasticity is at all fatal to the integrity of the concept but helps to define it as one involving variety), and it is difficult to define the beginning of any phenomenon historically. However, I think 1965 can be offered as a time from which to date its greatest development. That year embraces not only the first real growth of the underground press, leading to the founding of UPS in 1966, but also the publication of two books that are of seminal importance stylistically to the New Journalism: Truman Capote's *In Cold Blood* and Tom Wolfe's *The Kandy-Kolored Tangerine-Flake Streamline Baby.* The first had an ambiguous but significant impact on journalists as well as other literary artists, and the second was the beginning of the career of one of the most innovative, flamboyant, and copied journalistic geniuses of recent times.

TRUMAN CAPOTE

Truman Capote had experimented with techniques of reportage before he wrote *In Cold Blood,* but it was that book which made the most impact for change. With eight books already to his credit, Capote turned his main creative energy from writing fiction to writing a book-length novelistic account of a real event, calling into play the meticulous and precocious talent that had made him a major figure in fictional literature. The story of the murder of the Clutter family of Holcomb, Kansas, by Eugene Hickock and Perry Smith, was carefully reconstructed and filled out through extensive examinations of official records and long interviews with Hickock and Smith, people who knew the Clutters, and law officers involved in the case; and Capote lived in Kansas long enough to gain and present in his book a detailed and rich sense of the place of the murder. He also followed the prison lives of the two men until they were hanged, an experience which has led him to write for prison reform, a kind of reformation journalism he hopes to bring to television soon but can't presently because of the reluctance of producers to handle such touchy and revelatory material. In any case, *In Cold Blood* is an extremely well-researched book.

Capote's sense of place is remarkable, and it is central to his style and the truth of his journalism. Consider the opening of the book:

> The village of Holcomb stands on the high wheat plains of western Kansas, a lonesome area that other Kansans call "out there." Some seventy miles east of the Colorado border, the countryside, with its hard blue skies and desert-clear air, has an atmosphere that is rather more Far West than Middle West. The local accent is barbed with prairie twang, a ranch-hand nasalness, and the men, many of them, wear narrow frontier trousers, Stetsons, and high-heeled boots with pointed toes. The land is flat, and the views are awesomely extensive; horses, herds of cattle, a white cluster of grain elevators rising as gracefully as Greek temples are visible long before a traveler reaches them.[1]

The phenomenology is that of an outsider, but one keenly attuned to the moods resident in the place. Capote has selected details which are realistic, true to more traditional journalistic practice, but there is also an attendant and indirect symbology, perhaps, in the isolation and starkness of the landscape with grain elevators like Aeschylean temples.

There are other qualities of the book which exist because of the harmony of Capote's journalistic and novelistic purposes: the dialogue is utterly credible, derived as it is from the talk and memories of human experience; the characters are beautifully realized, largely because they as people are very important to Capote; the suspense developed as the author recounts the events leading to the convergence of the murderers and the Clutters gives the vitality of gut truth and mystery to a seemingly senseless act of violence, which, without Capote, the public would have known through standard reportage only as fragments and piecemeal facts or speculation, as "news." Through dialogue, character, and a mood of suspenseful fatality, Capote succeeds in escalating a numb pathos into a form of tragedy as valid as that of Arthur Miller. The delineation of the people involved, particularly Smith and Hickock, is not governed by any set of clichés about human personalities—whether of Kansans or homicidal maniacs—rather, Capote allows the reader to discover his characters, just as he discovered them as people. And Capote, true to his own novelistic esthetic, concludes the book with no quick judgment or summation, no easy drawing together of data for swollen indignation, and no flat resignation to fact. He tries, rather, to preserve an openness and compassion toward the executed murderers and their victims, to leave to the reader the act of moral assessment and tragic reconciliation, an act for which Capote has prepared him by expanding and formulating factual reportage until it reveals a mythic and deeply human event.

TOM WOLFE

If one of the remarkable qualities of Capote's journalism is the artistic restraint which allows him to build creatively around a central set of facts, something like the opposite is true of Tom Wolfe, whose baroque, effervescent, near-surrealistic style derives from his ability to let events reveal themselves as exploding, maniacal, and, usually, typically American. Wolfe's imaginative journalism bears the mark of his personality and style just as clearly as Capote's nonfictional novel bears the mark of his less personal but equally real genius.

Wolfe is a kind of poet-journalist, related in one direction to older writers like Ben Hecht, in another to the black humorists and experimental novelists like Don Barthelme and Thomas Pynchon. In some respects he is very much a pop artist, but in others he is obviously an extremely disciplined and accurate prose stylist like Gay Talese, by whom Wolfe claims he has been influenced.[2] More basically, he is an extremely good journalist with his own distinctive talent. His prose can be as clean and clear and traditionally articulate as that of George Orwell, or it can be as complex, syntactically labyrinthine, and semantically intuitive as that of Faulkner. His writing frequently resembles that of Norman Mailer in its quick cadences and rapid-fire illuminations, and he, like Mailer, is related to modern American journalist-writers such as Hemingway or Ring Lardner. Wolfe, again like Mailer, whom I shall discuss presently, has an uncanny ability to respond to the hidden and less obvious forces of events and phenomena, to see madness beneath the surface of accepted behavior, and to discern the allegorical and ritual significance, or the desperate absurdity, of human activity, whether it be everyday or extraordinary. However, it is the style of his writing, the manner of his journalistic presentation, which most distinguishes him as one of the best New Journalists.

The Kandy-Kolored Tangerine-Flake Streamline Baby is a collection of twenty-two pieces written over a fifteen-month period for the New York *Herald Tribune, Esquire,* and other journals and newspapers. Wolfe's introduction is an important document of the New Journalism, because it is a statement concerning why he changed his writing style. He was originally a "totem" journalist, and totem journalism is part of the accepted complacent life-style, as Wolfe says in his own remarkable way:

> A totem newspaper is the kind people don't really buy to read but just to *have,* physically, because they know it supports their own outlook on life. They're just like the buffalo tongues the Omaha Indians used to carry around or the dog ears the Mahili clan carried around in Bengal. There are two kinds of totem newspapers in the country. One is the symbol of the frightened chair-arm-doilie Vicks Vapo-Rub *Weltanschauung* that lies there in the solar plexus of all good gray burghers. All those nice stories on the first page of the second section about eighty-seven-year-old ladies on Gramercy Park who have one-hundred-and-two-year-old turtles or about the colorful street vendors of Havana. Mommy! This fellow Castro is in there, and revolutions may come and go, but the picturesque poor will endure, padding around in the streets selling their chestnuts and salt pretzels the world over, even in Havana, Cuba, assuring a paradise, after all, full of respect and obeisance, for all us Vicks Vapo-Rub chair-arm-doilie burghers. After all. Or another totem group buys the kind of paper they can put under their arms and have the totem for the tough-but-wholesome outlook, the Mom's Pie view of life. Everybody can go off to the bar and drink a few "brews" and retail some cynical remarks about Zora Folley and how the fight game is these days and round it off, though, with how George Chuvalo has "a lot of heart," which he got, one understands, by eating mom's pie.[3]

With this view of the established press stewing in his mind, Wolfe went to the Hot Rod and Custom Car Show at the Coliseum in New York to do a story for the *Herald Tribune*. He wrote a story "that would have suited any of the totem newspapers," a type of story which "usually makes what is known as 'gentle fun' of this, which is a way of saying, don't worry, these people are nothing." After he wrote the story, he was nagged by an awareness that there was another story he had not written, so he went to *Esquire* with an idea for it; and *Esquire* sent him to California for a closer look at the world of custom cars. After experiencing the car-culture world in Los Angeles, he returned to New York and tried to write his story:

> I had a lot of trouble analyzing exactly what I had on my hands. By this time *Esquire* practically had a gun at my head because they had a two-page-wide color picture for the story locked into the printing presses and no story. Finally, I told Byron Dobell, the managing editor at *Esquire*, that I couldn't pull the thing together. O.K., he tells me, just type out my notes and send them over and he will get somebody else to write it. So about 8 o'clock that night I started typing the notes out in the form of a memorandum that began, "Dear Byron." I started typing away, starting right with the first time I saw any custom cars in California. I just started recording it all, and inside of a couple of hours, typing along like a madman, I could tell that something was beginning to happen. By midnight this memorandum to Byron was twenty pages long and I was still typing like a maniac. About 2 A.M. or something like that I turned on WABC, a radio station that plays rock and roll music all night long, and got a little more manic. I wrapped up the memorandum about 6:15 A.M., and by this time it was 49 pages long. I took it over to *Esquire* as soon as they opened up, about 9:30 A.M. About 4 P.M. I got a call from Byron Dobell. He told me they were striking out the "Dear Byron" at the top of the memorandum and running the rest of it in the magazine. That was the story, "The Kandy-Kolored Tangerine-Flake Streamline Baby." (xiii-xiv)

Wolfe goes on to say that it was the "details themselves" of his experience that "made me see what was happening."

This title essay of the book is devoted to seeing customizing for what it really is—art—and the people for what they are—artists. The striking thing about his break with traditional journalism was the spontaneity of consciousness through which he began to deal with details and to spin out their significance—that is one of his talents as a writer. Also, from his account, one sees his commitment to getting close to, involved with, his subject, to talking to car-culture people and listening to their music when he wrote. It was necessary for Wolfe to participate fully in the culture he was writing about; and once he was attuned to the vibrations of that culture, his style had to change to accommodate its style, to do justice to it in his reporting. Perhaps only a young man, one as open, energetic, and richly educated as Wolfe himself, could have done it the way he did.

Once Wolfe found himself outside what he calls the old "system of ideas," the old journalistic conceptions of style, and the old clichés concerning what deserves the journalist's attention, he went on to explore other phenomena of pop culture and the metropolitan-neon life-styles of America. Besides the essay on car culture, there are twenty-one other pieces that exemplify the new Wolfe style; and there is also a short sketchbook of various New York types, such as cab drivers and ducktail-cultivators. The piece on stock-car champion Junior Johnson, "The Last American Hero," is a fast-paced account of a rural-technological hero who learned how to drive running illegal whiskey, performing daredevil stunts to evade tax agents, and whose life-style, through Wolfe's rich observation and electrical language, can be seen for what it really is—folk-mythic. There are also vignettes on Cary Grant, "Loverboy of the Bourgeoisie," and Cassius Clay, "The Marvelous Mouth," as well as pieces on such subjects as rock culture, disk jockeys, and the empty, ritualistic lives of young divorcees in New York.

A piece which is characteristic of Wolfe and reveals his baroque sense of color and cadence and his ability to suggest the depths beneath the surface of an accepted American institution is the one which opens the book, "Las Vegas (What?) Las Vegas (Can't hear you! Too noisy) Las Vegas!!!!":

> Such shapes! Boomerang Modern supports, Palette Curvilinear bars, Hot Shoppe Cantilever roofs and a scalloped swimming pool. Such colors! All the new electrochemical pastels of the Florida littoral: tangerine, broiling magenta,

livid pink, incarnadine, fuchsia demure, Congo ruby, methyl green, viridine, aquamarine, phenosafranine, incandescent orange, scarlet-fever purple, cyanic blue, tessellated bronze, hospital-fruit-basket orange. And such signs! Two cylinders rose at either end of the Flamingo—eight stories high and covered from top to bottom with neon rings in the shape of bubbles that fizzed all eight stories up into the desert sky all night long like an illuminated whiskey-soda tumbler filled to the brim with pink champagne. . . . The wheeps, beeps, freeps, electronic lulus, Boomerang Modern and Flash Gordon sunbursts soar on through the night over the billowing hernia-hernia sounds of the old babes at the slots—until it is 7:30 A.M. and I am watching five men at a green-topped card table playing poker. . . . But what is all this? Off to the side, at a rostrum, sits a flawless little creature with bouffant hair and Stridex-pure skin who looks like she is polished each morning with a rotary buffer. Before her on the rostrum is a globe of coffee on a hot coil. Her sole job is to keep the poker players warmed up with coffee. (9-10, 12, 13)

Wolfe's Las Vegas is everything everyone knows it is: corrupt, artificial, plastic, luxurious for those who want their "luxury" that way, a labyrinth of different kinds of prostitution, deceit, and callousness, in many ways an old-folks' home supplied with gaudy, tempting, empty beauty. But Wolfe's style also calls up its surrealism, its science-fictional presence in the center of a desert, and its flamboyant, desperate madness and absurdity. His vignettes of decrepit women cranking endlessly on slot machines, of people unable to relate to one another with any real humanity, and, most tellingly, of a mental patient cranking at an imaginary slot machine, portray Las Vegas as the neo-Boschian, very American, false but fascinating Sodom-Eden that it is. He renders it as a perfect Kafkaesque nightmare that intrigues and repells, and thus brings a literary esthetic to journalism without rendering his reportage any less "factual."

Tom Wolfe's work for various journals during the next three years was collected in *The Pump House Gang*, which was published in 1968 along with his book-length story of Ken Kesey and the Merry Pranksters, *The Electric Kool-Aid Acid Test*, part of which had been previously published by the now defunct *World Journal Tribune* in its Sunday magazine, *New*

York.[4] As both books show, Wolfe is continuously developing his new style and expanding his interest in pop culture to include all manner of strange aberrations and beautiful odysseys.

In *The Pump House Gang* Wolfe's awareness of cultural sickness forces his writing to betray occasionally some of the malaise of a new Ferdinand Céline, particularly in the title piece, about California surfing culture, where he reveals all too clearly the meanness of youth fascinated with its sun-tanned beauty; but most of the time he is typically inside his subject, watching it explode into its full madness and color. He is drunk on the variety and strangeness of the contemporary world, but he is also creatively in control of his recording of it. In the introduction he speaks of his rapid writing, traveling, and data-gathering:

> I wrote all but two of these stories in one ten-month stretch after the publication of my first book, *The Kandy-Kolored Tangerine-Flake Streamline Baby.* It was a strange time for me. Many rogue volts of euphoria. I went from one side of this country to the other and then from one side of England to the other. The people I met—the things they did—I was entranced. I met Carol Doda. She blew up her breasts with emulsified silicone, the main ingredient in Silly Putty, and became the greatest resource of the San Francisco tourist industry. I met a group of surfers, the Pump House Gang. They attended the Watts riot as if it were the Rose Bowl in Pasadena. They came to watch "the drunk niggers" and were reprimanded by the same for their rowdiness. In London I met a competitive 17-year-old named Nicki who got one-up on her schoolgirl chums by taking a Kurdish clubfoot lover. I met a £9-a-week office boy named Larry Lynch. He spent his lunch hour every day with hundreds of other child laborers in the crazed pitchblack innards of a noonday nightclub called Tiles. All of them in *ecstasis* from the frug, the rock 'n' roll, and God knows what else, for an hour—then back to work. In Chicago I met Hugh Hefner. He revolved on his bed, offering scenic notes as his head floated by—. (1)

All of those people and events populate and fill out the book, along with many others, including Marshall McLuhan (featured in a fantastic satirical drawing which prefaces "What If

He Is Right?") and anthropologist Edward T. Hall ("O Rotten Gotham—Sliding Down into the Behavorial Sink"). There is also a satirical foray into manners in "Tom Wolfe's New Book of Etiquette."

If there is a Céline mood in some of Wolfe's writing, it is usually short-circuited by his depression-transcending dramatization of events through a highly rhetorical style; but there is a complex comic-serious aspect to almost all of his writing. "The Pump House Gang" is a case in point. At the opening of the piece, Wolfe oscillates deftly between a journalistic account of place and the psychological point of view of the surfers, the style revealing the meditation of his own consciousness. It is a pop composition with pathetic overtones:

> Our boys never hair out. The black panther has black feet. Black feet on the crumbling black panther. Panthuh. Mee-dah. Pam Stacy, 16 years old, a cute girl here in La Jolla, California, with a pair of orange bell-bottom hip-huggers on, sits on a step about four steps down the stairway to the beach and she can see a pair of revolting black feet without lifting her head. So she says it out loud, "The black panther."
>
> Somebody farther down the stairs, one of the boys with the *major* hair and khaki shorts, says, "The black feet of the black panther."
>
> "Mee-dah," says another kid. This happens to be the cry of a, well, *underground* society known as the Mac Meda Destruction Company.
>
> "The pan-thuh."
>
> "The poon-thuh."
>
> All these kids, seventeen of them, members of the Pump House crowd, are lollygagging around the stairs down to Windansea Beach, La Jolla, California, about 11 A.M., and they all look at the black feet, which are a woman's pair of black street shoes, out of which stick a pair of old veiny white ankles, which lead up like a senile cone to a fudge of tallowy, edematous flesh, her thighs, squeezing out of her bathing suit, with old faded yellow bruises on them, which she probably got from running eight feet to catch a bus or something. (15)

Wolfe has recorded some of the psychological pain of the

generation gap in this *cinéma vérité* sort of sequence, and he has caught the lingo of the surfers, their arrogance and attitudes more truly than any standard reportage could.

He opens the piece much as a novelist or short-story writer would, carefully composing the setting, the characters, the dialogue, subtly presenting a condensation of the themes and conflicts to follow, foreshadowing the end of his story; and the end, after Wolfe has taken us through the beauty and inhumanity of the surfing world, comes with a sterile homicide-suicide and a final resurfacing to the now-transformed mood of the piece's beginning:

—the panthers scrape on up the sidewalk. They are at just about the point Leonard Anderson and Donna Blanchard got that day, December 6, 1964, when Leonard said, Pipe it, and fired two shots, one at her and one at himself. Leonard was 18 and Donna was 21—21!—god, for a girl in the Pump House gang that is almost the horror line right there. But it was all so mysterioso. Leonard was just lying down on the beach at the foot of the Pump House, near the stairs, just talking to John K. Weldon down there, and then Donna appeared at the top of the stairs and Leonard got up and went up the stairs to meet her, and they didn't say anything, they weren't *angry* over anything, they never had been, although the police said they had, they just turned and went a few feet down the sidewalk, away from the Pump House and—blam blam!—these two shots. Leonard fell dead on the sidewalk and Donna died that afternoon in Scripps Memorial Hospital. Nobody knew what to think. But one thing it seemed like —well, it seemed like Donna and Leonard thought they had lived *The Life* as far as it would go and now it was running out. All that was left to do was—but that is an *insane* idea. It can't be like that, *The Life* can't run out, people can't change all that much just because godsown chronometer runs on and the body packing starts deteriorating and the fudgy tallow shows up at the thighs where they squeeze out of the bathing suit—

Tom, boy! John, boy! Gary, boy! Neale, boy! Artie, boy! Pam, Liz, Vicki, Jackie Haddad! After all this —just a pair of bitchin black panther bunions inching down the sidewalk away from the old Pump House stairs? (30)

This style of New Journalistic writing has a literary merit all its own, as does that of Capote, in the use of language for recreating human realities. Wolfe's use of irony is itself an entire mode of journalistic commentary, and his thematic capitulation at the end is very effective, as is the theatrical curtain call, in giving the reader a total sense of the story to which he, through Wolfe, has been a witness. Wolfe has combined comedy and poignancy in a brilliant fashion. As Raymond Mungo said of the underground press, he has transcended facts, perhaps sometimes carelessly (we are never sure Wolfe is on the scene for everything he reports), but he has told the truth; and he has told it by using the facts as a foundation for a creative and always in some way personal journalism.

In *The Electric Kool-Aid Acid Test* Wolfe turns from the maniacal new fetishes and religions of the larger pop culture of the affluent society to those of Ken Kesey and the Merry Pranksters, a commune of beautiful freaks on the ambiguous fringe of the future. This book-length story is already a classic. Like Capote's *In Cold Blood,* but in an entirely different key, it is really an experimental nonfiction novel more than anything else, and also perhaps the best single work of New Journalism to date. The only work comparable to it since *In Cold Blood* is Norman Mailer's *The Armies of the Night,* also published in 1968. *Acid Test* is full of psychosociological insights, but the reader experiences the story with a fast-paced involvement that is reminiscent of Jack Kerouac's *On the Road,* a book which may well have influenced Wolfe. In fact, *Acid Test* is a vision of hippie culture in roughly the same way that *On the Road* was a vision of the beat culture of the 1950's, although Wolfe's book is better written, and written with a different set of purposes. Although involved with the people of his book, Wolfe is also detached, skeptical, and sometimes writes through a broad esthetic-historical overview. As a result of his shifting point of view, he is more willing to see comedy and absurdity than Kerouac was, but both books have a vision of the tragedy of their respective cultures and are closely attuned through style to the feverishness of people living out new and sometimes desperate life-experiments in order to transcend the sickness of their age.

A summary of Wolfe's story, insofar as it can be summarized, would be helpful before discussing his style, because his style grows out of the fantastic events of the story. Kesey came originally from Oregon. Before writing two brilliant and original novels, *One Flew Over the Cuckoo's Nest* (1962) and *Sometimes a Great Notion* (1964), he volunteered as a guinea pig for drug experiments at the Veterans Hospital in Menlo Park, California, in 1959. Through these experiments he became fascinated with the possibilities of mind-expanding drugs, particularly LSD; he took them and embarked into a new universe. Gradually he gathered around him a group of people who named themselves the Merry Pranksters. He was a sort of psychedelic shaman-chieftain-wizard of the tribe, and his life became for them a kind of futuristic folk myth in which they all participated—a situation somewhat similar to that of Valentine Michael Smith and his commune in Robert Heinlein's now-classic *Stranger in a Strange Land*. Then, in 1964, the Pranksters rebuilt an old school bus, giving it a 400-horsepower engine. They installed an elaborate maze of Ampex electronic recording equipment, movie cameras, and projectors; painted the bus in mind-blowing patterns with Day-Glo paint; and took off across America with an ample cache of LSD.

The entire happening became known as the "movie." Everyone was to keep his feelings "out front" and, within vague boundaries, "do his own thing." The world of man was divided into those who were "on the bus" and those who weren't. This rolling science-fiction-movie Esalen Institute went across the United States to Timothy Leary's commune at Milbrook, New York, and back to California, with the participants dropping acid, filming, and recording everything that happened. Back home after that $103,000 Magical Mystery Tour, which Kesey himself financed, the tribe joined with the Grateful Dead rock group, Hell's Angels (whom they may have changed, some small bit, for the better), and anyone else who would come, to give the Acid Tests. The Tests, sometimes featuring acid, sometimes not, were beautiful, sometimes catastrophic, psychedelic celebrations featuring rock music, light shows, stroboscopic dancing, and any spontaneous thing that happened; and they set the style for all the hippie culture that followed. After that came Kesey's fleeing to Mexico and back because of drug charges, his arrest, his release after five months, and his return to Oregon, where the story ends.

The Electric Kool-Aid Acid Test is first and foremost a book in which Wolfe has tried to communicate through the use of language his various and complex *feelings* about the activities of Kesey and the Pranksters. From the time he meets Kesey coming out of jail at the first of the book, through the odyssey of the bus across the country and back to California, until Kesey's return to his home state of Oregon at the end, Wolfe is trying to keep the reader tuned to the sense of events, to tell "what it was like"; and yet his own mediation always enters at just the right point to speculate, to expand, or, usually very subtly, to judge. Wolfe's description of part of the bus ride, the central activity of the book, represents some of his best writing and illustrates clearly how his style is close to the events he describes:

> And they went with the flow, the whole goddam flow of America. The bus barrels into the superhighway toll sta- tions and the microphones on top of the bus pick up all the clacking and ringing and the mumbling by the toll- station attendant and the brakes squeaking and the gears shifting, all the sounds of the true America that are screened out everywhere else, it all came amplified back inside the bus, while Hagen's camera picked up the faces, the faces in Phoenix, the cops, the service-station owners, the stragglers and the strugglers of America, all laboring in their movie, and it was all captured and kept, piling up, inside the bus. Barreling across America with the microphones picking it all up, the whole roar, and the microphone up top gets eerie in a great rush and then *skakkkkkkkkkkkkkk* it is ripping and roaring over asphalt and *thok* it's gone, no sound at all. The microphone has somehow ripped loose on top of the bus and hit the road- way and dragged along until it snapped off entirely—and Sandy can't believe it. He keeps waiting for somebody to tell Cassady to stop and go back and get the microphone, because this was something Sandy had rigged up with great love and time, it was his *thing*, his part of the power—but instead they are all rapping and grokking over the sound it made—"Wowwwwwwwwww! Did you— wowwwwwwww"—as if they had synched into a never- before-heard thing, a unique thing, the sound of an object, a microphone, hitting the American asphalt, the open road at 70 miles an hour, like if it was all there on tape

they would have the instant, the moment, of anything, *anyone* ripped out of the flow and hitting the Great Super-highway at 70 miles an hour—and they *had* it on tape—and played it back in variable lag skakkkkkk-akkk-akkkk-akkkoooooooooooo.

oooooooooooooooooooooooo—Stark Naked waxing weirder and weirder, huddled in the black blanket shivering, then out, bobbing wraith, her little deep red aureola bobbing in the crazed vibrations—finally they pull into Houston and head for Larry McMurtry's house. They pull up to McMurtry's house, in the suburbs, and the door of the house opens and out comes McMurtry, a slight, slightly wan, kindly-looking shy-looking guy, ambling out, with his little boy, his son, and Cassady opens the door of the bus so everybody can get off, and suddenly Stark Naked shrieks out: "Frankie! Frankie! Frankie! Frankie!"—this being the name of her own divorced-off little boy—and she whips off the blanket and leaps off the bus and out into the suburbs of Houston, Texas, stark naked, and rushes up to McMurtry's little boy and scoops him up and presses him to her skinny breast, crying and shrieking, "Frankie! oh Frankie! my little Frankie! oh! oh! oh!"—while Mc-Murtry doesn't know what in the name of hell to do, reaching tentatively toward her stark-naked shoulder and saying, "Ma'am! Ma'am! Just a minute, ma'am!"—

—while the Pranksters, spilling out of the bus—stop. The bus is stopped. No roar, no crazed bounce or vibrations, no crazed car beams, no tapes, no microphones. Only Stark Naked, with somebody else's little boy in her arms, is bouncing and vibrating.

And there, amid the peaceful Houston elms on Quenby Road, it dawned on them all that this woman—which one of us even knows her?—had completed her trip. She had gone with the flow. She had gone stark raving mad. (75-77)

This two-page description of the bus ride leading up to Stark Naked's freak-out is a sketch of the movement of the whole book, the whole Kesey-Prankster experiment, through ecstasy to disillusionment, though not negation. The technique of the book is also paralleled here: the winding up to a frenetic pitch of word-flow and involvement, followed by a rapid slowing down to the language and attitude of assessment.

The passage shows all the marks of Wolfe's journalistic style, as well as the ambiguity as to whether or not he was there, as to how close he was to the experience he has so beautifully recreated. His use of onomatopoeia is fun to experience and very effective in creating the all-important feeling of the event. Hip terminology is brought freely into play, and it is tremendously effective as a device for staying close to the thought patterns of his people. At the end of the passage he has the reader totally identified with their point of view. The dramatic punctuations and emphases push the prose into strong rhythmic cadences until the grinding flatness of the end, where Wolfe has finally played out the suggestions of horror in the word *stark*, with its suggestions of the vulnerability of human beings when encountering extreme experiences nakedly. And the rhetorical sweep of his long sentences pulls together all the fragments of the experience into a kaleidoscopic whole. What Wolfe has attempted in the *Acid Test* is the fullest possible re-creation of a story by a revolutionary journalistic style, and in large measure he has succeeded beautifully—an end to be envied by any journalist, no matter what his style.

In a review of Tom Wolfe's *Pump House Gang* and *Acid Test,* Robert Scholes formulates some suggestive thoughts about the kind of writing I am calling New Journalism, and he makes some helpful distinctions between the writing of Wolfe and that of Norman Mailer, to whom I will turn next. Scholes observes that our age is a hysterical one and that, therefore, such writers as Wolfe and Mailer, with their meticulous recording of its symptoms, should be called "hystorians," an idea which has to do with their journalistic style:

> The so-called stylistic excesses of such men as Norman Mailer and Tom Wolfe are in my view no more than the indispensable equipment they must employ in doing justice to our times. This is not to say that one must himself be hysterical to chronicle hysteria, but to suggest that hysteria cannot be assimilated and conveyed by one who is totally aloof. Mailer and Wolfe are not hysterical but they manage to remain more open to the contemporary scene than most reporters or commentators. They are more involved in what they report than a journalist would be,

and they bring to their reporting a more efficient intellectual apparatus, a richer framework of ideas and attitudes, a perspective more historical than journalistic.

I mention both Mailer and Wolfe because together they suggest the vigor and variety of this modern literary form which applies the imaginative resources of fiction to the world around us. The old realistic novel in its death throes is fragmenting into two new forms—a more fabulous nonrealistic fiction and an imaginative literature freed of the necessity to invent stories, a creative journalism that I am calling hystory.

The hystorian operates differently from the orthodox journalist. Perhaps the credulous believe that a reporter reports facts and that newspapers print all of them that are fit to print. But actually newspapers print all the "facts" that fit, period—that fit the journalistic conventions of what "a story" is (those tired formulas) and that fit the editorial policy of the paper. The hystorian fights this tendency toward formula with his own personality. He asserts the importance of *his* impression and *his* vision of the world. He embraces the fictional element inevitable in any reporting and tries to imagine his way toward the truth, instead of allowing the clichés of journalism to shape assembled facts into "news."

. . . Though both men are stylists, Mailer's style is a projection of his personality, which occupies the foreground of his book. Wolfe's chameleon styles are more reflective of his material than of himself. In fact, the two men represent two quite distinct reactions to the contemporary scene. Mailer is engaged, political, ethical. Wolfe is detached, social, esthetic. Mailer has affinities with the activists of the New Left; Wolfe is closer to the hippies and acid heads that are dropping out. Mailer is interested in probing depths, Wolfe in exploring surfaces. Mailer's concern is morals, Wolfe's manners. Mailer's hystory has a tragic and apocalyptic dimension; Wolfe's is essentially comic and Epicurean.[5]

I think Scholes is right when he says that this writing is a new form of literature, and "New Journalism," in the stylistic sense, may well be a broad term for a new literary genre. Certainly the work of Capote, Wolfe, and Mailer supports his speculation, and so does much of the writing of the underground-press journalists, as well as that of other writers, as we shall see in the following chapters. His observations concerning the journalistic style and attitudes toward reportage of the New Journalists lend support to my own, and the distinctions he makes between the writing of Mailer and Wolfe, whether or not one agrees with them completely, will be helpful to keep in mind in the discussion that follows.

NORMAN MAILER

Besides being a novelist, Norman Mailer has done a great deal of journalistic writing in the last fifteen years. Much of his writing for *Esquire* and other magazines during the early 1960's was in the vanguard of good journalistic writing. The earliest piece which foreshadows clearly his leaning toward the New Journalism he helped to found is "Superman Comes to the Supermarket," a report on Kennedy's candidacy published by *Esquire* in November of 1960; and one may find other examples in *The Presidential Papers of Norman Mailer* (1963) or in other collections of his work, such as *Cannibals and Christians* (1966). However, it was his 90,000-word piece, "The Steps of the Pentagon," concerning the Pentagon demonstration in October 1967, published in *Harper's*, March 1968, that marked his coming of age as a New Journalist. It, along with his more objective history of and final reflections on the demonstration, "The Battle of the Pentagon," published in *Commentary*, April 1968, was published later that year in book form as *The Armies of the Night*.

In the subtitle of the book Mailer describes his purpose: *History as a Novel, The Novel as History,* an idea which aligns him with Capote and Wolfe as a genre-maker. Unlike Capote and Wolfe, he features himself as the novel's neo-Jamesian perceiver and Mailerian protagonist, speaking of this character in a self-conscious third person as "Mailer." What Mailer writes of concerning the Pentagon demonstration is not simply the event itself but also the larger aberrations and motivations of the American psyche he sees operating there, a task he had undertaken earlier through the electronic-scatological metaphors of his novel *Why Are We in Vietnam?* (1967). Having pushed a fictional exploration of the contemporary American psyche about as far as he could in that book, he turned his energies to the larger, perhaps more complex task of exploring the activities of that psyche, and of his own, in the frenetic reality of events: history is the raw material of the novelist's art; and the novel is essentially a historical-narrative or, here, journalistic genre.

"History as a Novel: The Steps of the Pentagon," the first part of the book, is concerned with the activities of the demonstration itself: the parties and speeches beforehand, the Lincoln Memorial rally, the herd-like march across the Potomac by way of one crowded bridge, the taunting of the guard around the Pentagon and on top of the machine-gun-armed building, the arrests of those (including Mailer) who attempted to storm the guard lines, the night in jail—all told with the immediacy, breath-taking cadence, and symbolic sense of detail one associates with Mailer's writing. And through it all Mailer is honest and confessional about his feeling toward the people and the events they were creating. His portraits of Dwight MacDonald, Paul Goodman, Robert Lowell, and other personages involved are memorable, accurate, and revealing of both Mailer and his subjects, for his jealousies and dislikes come freely into play. He says of Robert Lowell, for instance, that he "gave off at times the unwilling haunted saintliness of a man who was repaying the moral debts of ten generations of ancestors"[6]—a description which catches him exactly and at the same time reveals subtly some of Mailer's uneasiness about the greatness of Lowell's talent.

Also, though their styles differ in many ways, Mailer resembles Wolfe in his ability to recreate the feeling, the mythical and psychological ambience, of an event. As an example, consider his description of the gathering before the Lincoln Memorial:

> And from the north and the east, from the direction of the White House and the Smithsonian and the Capitol, from Union Station and the Department of Justice the troops were coming in, the volunteers were answering the call. They came walking up in all sizes, a citizens' army not ranked yet by height, an army of both sexes in numbers almost equal, and of all ages, although most were young. Some were well-dressed, some were poor, many were con-

ventional in appearance, as often were not. The hippies were there in great number, perambulating down the hill, many dressed like the legions of Sgt. Pepper's Band, some were gotten up like Arab sheiks, or in Park Avenue's doormen's greatcoats, others like Rogers and Clark of the West, Wyatt Earp, Kit Carson, Daniel Boone in buckskin, some had grown mustaches to look like *Have Gun, Will Travel*—Paladin's surrogate was here!—and wild Indians with feathers, a hippie gotten up like Batman, another like Claude Rains in *The Invisible Man*—his face wrapped in a turban of bandages and he wore a black satin top hat. (108)

Or he can communicate very effectively the pressure and presence of the crowd and the close, physical character of the event, as in this passage where the demonstration moves from Lincoln Memorial to cross the Arlington Memorial Bridge:

Picture then this mass, bored for hours by speeches, now elated at the beginning of the March, now made irritable by delay, now compressed, all old latent pips of claustrophobia popping out of the crush, and picture them as they stepped out toward the bridge, monitors in the lead, hollow square behind, next the line of notables with tens, then hundreds of lines squeezing up behind, helicopters overhead, police gunning motorcycles, cameras spinning their gears like the winging of horseflies, TV car bursting seams with hysterically overworked technicians, sun beating overhead—this huge avalanche of people rumbled forward thirty feet and came to a stop in disorder, the lines breaking and warping and melding into themselves to make a crowd not a parade, and some jam-up at the front, just what no one knew, now they were moving again. Forty more feet. They stopped. At this rate it would take six hours to reach the Pentagon. And a murmur came up from behind of huge discontent, not huge yet, huge in the potential of its discontent. "Let's get going," people in the front lines were calling out. (126)

Both passages have a cinematic, or TV-camera, kind of visual presence, with the addition of imagination in the first and a sense of strain and impatience in the second.

Mailer shifts from the excited narration of events into long reflective passages with ease, apologizing that it is "One of the oldest devices of the novelist" (152); and these passages, feverishly insightful, usually derive directly from and illuminate magically the described event they follow. After telling of his wait on the police bus following his arrest, Mailer ascends into the rich, sweeping, metaphorical style, the driving cadences and moral quandaries of *Why Are We in Vietnam?* The Arnoldian overtones of the title begin to be explored: why do men wage war; why this particular war, that must be opposed by the "armies" of the humane and conscientious? For Mailer, the war in Vietnam, like the Pentagon demonstration and his own way of perceiving and recording it, is peculiarly American and must be seen in that way, as it was in *Why Are We in Vietnam?* His reportage of his arrest leads him to darker thoughts:

> One did not have to look for who would work in the concentration camps and the liquidation centers—the garrison would be filled with applicants from the pages of a hundred American novels, from *Day of the Locust* and *Naked Lunch* and *The Magic Christian,* one could enlist half the marshals outside this bus, simple, honest, hardworking government law-enforcement agents, yeah! There was something at loose now in American life, the poet's beast slinking to the marketplace. The country had always been wild. It had always been harsh and hard, it had always had a fever—when life in one American town grew insupportable, one could travel, the fever to travel was in the American blood, so said all, but now the fever had left the blood, it was in the cells, the cells traveled, and the cells were as insane as Grandma with orange hair [from a reference previously to a senile Las Vegas type—reminiscent of Wolfe]. The small towns were disappearing in the by-passes and the supermarkets and the shopping centers, the small town in America was losing its sense of the knuckle, the herb, and the root, the walking sticks were no longer cut from trees, nor were they cured, the schools did not have crazy old teachers now but teaching aids, and in the libraries, *National Geographic* gave way to *TV Guide.* . . . the American small town grew out of itself. . . . It had grown out of itself again and again, its cells trav-

eled, worked for government, found security through wars in foreign lands, and the nightmares which passed on the winds in the old small towns now traveled on the nozzle tip of the flame thrower, no dreams now of barbarian lusts, slaughtered villages, battles of blood, no, nor any need for them—technology had driven insanity out of the wind and out of the attic, and out of all the lost primitive places: one had to find it now wherever fever, force, and machines could come together, in Vegas, at the race track, in pro football, race riots for the Negro, suburban orgies—none of it was enough—one had to find it in Vietnam; that was where the small town had gone to get its kicks. (172-174)

This line of commentary comes to a head later in the first part: "He came to the saddest conclusion of them all for it went beyond the war in Vietnam. He had come to decide that the center of America might be insane" (211).

Mailer's journalism, as can be seen from the passages above, is frequently poetic, and that poetic quality sharpens the edge of his observations and speculations, giving them the vitality of a dawning consciousness in the reader. Faustian-Falstaffian Mailer uses the poetry as a kind of electricity to charge the described events with the significance and energy they had when originally experienced and to transform them into a central mythology of the present age. The effectiveness of *The Armies of the Night* as journalism is due largely to Mailer's remarkable ability to combine poetry and objectivity into a greater whole. In the reportage of the first part he retains a heuristic, exploratory attitude throughout, so that by the time he finishes "History as a Novel: The Steps of the Pentagon," he is "delivered a discovery of what the March on the Pentagon had finally meant" and so is ready "to write a most concise Short History, a veritable précis of a collective novel, which here now, in the remaining pages, will seek as History, no, rather as some Novel of History, to elucidate the mysterious character of that Quintessentially American event" (241).

The second part of the book, "The Novel as History: The Battle of the Pentagon," considerably shorter than the first, is a more objective piece. It narrates the history of preparation for the march and many events of which Mailer learned but had not directly experienced, including some of the "battles" between Pentagon guards and demonstrators which resulted in an incredible lot of brutality and arrests, as well as some touching moments of communication between the guards and the people demonstrating. Mailer's analysis of events leads to criticisms about the demonstration and how it might have been better handled, and the conclusion is a bleak portrait of America's sickness and totalitarianism. It is a much less personal document than the first part, less poetic, and to that extent more conventionally journalistic. However, Mailer strikes another blow for New Journalism in his criticism of the established press's reportage of the event as inaccurate, insensitive, and politically biased. When he wants reliable newspaper reporting for evidence in constructing his history, he turns to the Washington *Free Press*, an underground paper, not the Washington *Post* or *Time*, although he does find the Washington *Star* accurate at one point. Indeed, returning to the beginning of the first part of the book, one remembers that Mailer began his narrative with a report from *Time* of his own predemonstration speech in Washington's Ambassador Theater, asserting, after quoting *Time*'s report, that what followed would be "what happened" in reality (14). So the whole book is an attempt to give to the public the kind of coverage Mailer knew the established press would never offer, and the second part is to a great extent an attempt to correct the so-called "objectivity" of that press's reportage.

The first part is essential to the second, for through it we know the character of the journalist-historian of the second; we know what he has experienced, what he has not, and how he responds to what he experiences:

> So the Novelist working in secret collaboration with the Historian has perhaps tried to build with his novel a tower fully equipped with telescopes to study—at the greatest advantage—our own horizon. Of course, the tower is crooked, and the telescopes warped, but the instruments of all sciences—history so much as physics—are always constructed in small or large error; what supports the use of them now is that our intimacy with the master builder of the tower, and the lens grinder of the telescopes (yes, even the machinist of the barrels) has given some advantage for correcting the error of the instruments and the imbalance of his tower. May that be claimed of many histories? . . .

The method is then exposed. The mass media which surrounded the March on the Pentagon created a forest of inaccuracy which would blind the efforts of an historian; our novel has provided us with the possibility, no, even the instrument to view our facts and conceivably study them in that field of light a labor of lens-grinding has produced. (245-246)

That is Mailer's esthetic. It is primarily a historical and artistic esthetic, and it is one that is a key to the success of much of the New Journalism. It involves a bringing into play of the full power of the reporter's imagination and sensibility as essential to anything like an honest and relevant, if necessarily imperfect, journalism.

In *Miami and the Siege of Chicago* (1968) Mailer continues his examination of the American psyche, again in a political context, the most obvious one of all—the conventions. He subtitles the book *An Informal History of the Republican and Democratic Conventions of 1968*. Declaring in the first part, "Nixon in Miami," that New York *Times* reporters are not instructed that "there is no history without nuance,"[7] Mailer discloses his approach: he is writing a history *with* nuance, watching for, recording, and assessing the significance of gestures, peripheral events (as well as central ones), and attitudes. Stylistically, this book is similar to *The Armies of the Night,* which was also a "history with nuance." Again Mailer reveals his keen eyes for details, his ability to react to those details and to communicate his reactions vividly, accurately, openly, and, frequently, with poetic grace and depth. However, *Miami and the Siege of Chicago* is journalistically more like "The Battle of the Pentagon" than the first part of the previous book, for Mailer is less introspective and exhibitionistic. Identifying himself as "the reporter," he tries to be objective and interpretive, although he does, occasionally, inject personal reflections, particularly those concerning his sense of political affiliation as an evaluation of events. Thus, he shifts from a conservative radical role to that of a kind of cultural aristocrat, through others, until, after the Chicago convention he speculates that he wouldn't cast his vote—"not unless it was for Eldridge Cleaver" (223). He is trying to narrate honestly the changes of political attitude any man experiences in witnessing the conventions.

At any rate, this is probably the best report of the 1968 conventions in print.

Mailer's rapid writing—this book took two weeks—and his heuristic-dialectic manner of imaginatively feeling his way through events give his work a fantastic immediacy, as if the reader were embarked with him on a frenetic voyage of discovery, where the final boundaries, the settled character of things, can't be fully assessed—a task which is left to the stodgy historians of the future; what we are experiencing on the voyage, as Scholes says, is "hystory," something maniacally of the moment, uncertain, and difficult to document. Mailer's style, which is a product of a desire to pull together the telling facts of a situation, of a genius for transfiguring those facts into truth, and of a habit of writing rapidly, holding slow intellection to a minimum, is his secret as a writer; and, as Peter Shaw notes in his review of *Miami and the Siege of Chicago*, it links him to a classical tradition in American writing—which suggests some more of the historical roots of the New Journalism:

> Writing at high speed, he has time only to comprehend people and events imaginatively, in the novelist's way. As it turns out, in the frenetic form of the last two books, Mailer has found for himself a way to approximate the accomplishments of the classic American writers. They too had much to fear from giving a subject too much thought. Brooders like Hawthorne, Melville, and Mark Twain knew that they could destroy themselves and their work with too much intellection, and Hawthorne took that danger for the theme of many of his stories, in which excessive brooders destroyed their own works of art and even their loved ones.
>
> When we think of the great achievements in American writing we tend to think of symbolism and fantasy, of the romantic and the farfetched: the white whale, the dream world of Huckleberry Finn and Jim on the magic river, Hawthorne's dark puritan forests of symbols. But the other side of the American imagination has been just as important in its very different function of dealing with facts in order somehow to illuminate them. Mailer is not the first American novelist to revel in the role of reporter, gatherer of facts. I am thinking not only of Stephen Crane and Ernest Hemingway, but of the other side of *Moby*

Dick and *Huckleberry Finn* themselves, where not fantasy but *things* reign. Even more to the point, for Mailer's is a book about Chicago and about hotels, is Dreiser, who also could breathe life into the dross of America's gilt existence.[8]

I think Shaw's observation about the writer's, or Mailer's, attempt to avoid "brooding," over-intellection (not to say he doesn't think intelligently), or self-consciousness is quite true. That attempt is central to the salvation of literary art, including good journalism, in an incredibly self-conscious age. Mailer's shifting around of his protagonist's roles, of narrator identities, from "Mailer" to "the reporter" to "Aquarius" in his more recent work for *Life, Of a Fire on the Moon*, is an indication of his desire to avoid becoming too self-consciously present in his work—although, in a way, it makes him more so. Also, he clearly wants to avoid freezing his exploratory attitude into any kind of dogmatism; he wants to keep his ideas free, changing, his mind open to the forces of the moment. He wants, in short, to be a journalist, not a philosopher.

In "Nixon in Miami," the first part of *Miami and the Siege of Chicago*, Mailer tries to give life and significance to what was "the dullest convention anyone could remember" (15), and in many ways he succeeds beautifully, primarily because of his ability to see its placid events for what they really were: emblems of the vagaries of the American psyche. Consider, for example, his reportage of the place of the convention as an allegory of the Republican mentality:

> . . . the Republicans, Grand Old Party with a philosophy rather than a program, had chosen what must certainly be the materialist capital of the world for their convention. Las Vegas might offer competition, but Las Vegas was materialism in the service of electricity—fortunes could be in the spark of the dice. Miami was materialism baking in the sun, then stepping back to air-conditioned caverns where ice could nestle in the fur. It was the first of a hundred curiosities—that in a year when the Republic hovered on the edge of revolution, nihilism, and lines of police on the edge of the horizon, visions of future Vietnams in our own cities upon us, the party of conservatism and principle, of corporate wealth and personal frugality,

the party of cleanliness, hygiene, and balanced budget, should have set down on a sultan's strip. (14)

The emblematic character of the convention and its irrelevant curiosities have changed the mood of the narrator from what it was at the Pentagon. Less boisterous and self-displaying, "the reporter" moves through the convention "quietly, as anonymously as possible, wan, depressed, troubled" (14).

This is not an event which obviously and typically attracts his energies, but one in which he must learn to discern the ambiguous subtleties beneath the clean, boring surface. Mailer's observations of people are extremely careful, even if heuristic and inconclusive. His portrait of Nixon at a press conference, for instance, reveals a complex range of feelings and suspicions, and it is accurate:

> There was something in his carefully shaven face—the dark jowls already showing the first overtones of thin gloomy blue at this early hour—some worry which gave promise of never leaving him, some hint of inner debate about his value before eternity which spoke of precisely the sort of improvement that comes upon a man when he shifts in appearance from looking like an undertaker's assistant to looking like an old con seriously determined to go respectable. The Old Nixon, which is to say the young Nixon, used to look, on clasping his hands in front of him, like a church usher (of the variety who would twist a boy's ear after removing him from church). The older Nixon before the Press now—the *new* Nixon—had finally acquired some of the dignity of the old athlete and the old con—. . . . (44)

Gaining a sense of the convention's place, of Nixon and the other candidates, of the delegates and their gatherings, Mailer moves to a point where he begins to discern the importance of Nixon and his followers and, on the basis of his observations, formulates some journalistic speculations which have since been proven true prophecy:

> How could there be, after all, a greater passion in a man like Nixon, so universally half-despised, than to show the center of history itself that he was not without greatness. What a dream for such a man! . . . It was possible, even

likely, even necessary, that the Wasp must enter the center of our history again. . . . They were the most powerful force in America, and yet they were a psychic island. If they did not find a bridge, they could only grow more insane each year, like a rich nobleman in an empty castle chasing elves and ogres with his stick. They had every power but the one they needed—which was to attach their philosophy to history. . . . One could predict: their budgeting would prove insane, their righteousness would prove insane, their love for order and clear-thinking would be twisted through many a wry neck, the intellectual foundations of their anti-Communism would split into its separate parts. And the small-town faith in small free enterprise would run smash into the corporate juggernauts of technology land; their love of polite culture would collide with the mad esthetics of the new America; their livid passion for military superiority would smash its nose on the impossibility of having such superiority without more government spending; their love of nature would have to take up arms against the despoiling foe, themselves, their own greed, their own big business. (62-63)

If the event itself was dull and largely uneventful, Mailer's journalistic style and vision made it, at least, prophetic. The convention was also a kind of strange comedy, a fact which Mailer illustrates occasionally, partly by noticing its comic aspects, partly through a style of writing reminiscent of Wolfe's comic-esthetic point of view but colored with a moral darkness:

> At large on the ocean, would people yet pray for Nixon and wish him strength as once they had wished strength to old Hindenburg and Dollfuss and Schuschnigg and Von Papen? Oom-pah went the tuba, starts! went the horn. Blood and shit might soon be flying like the red and brown of a *verboten* flag. It had had black in it as well. For death perhaps. Areas of white for purity. They would talk yet of purity. They always did. And shave the shorn. God give strength to Richard Nixon, and a nose for the real news. Oom-pah went the tuba, *farts* went the horn. (66)

Perhaps the comedy itself was the prophecy, and Mailer left

Miami for Chicago with "no idea at all if God was in the land or the Devil played the tune" (82).

The second part, "The Siege of Chicago," opens with a portrait of Chicago. Mailer conjures up the aura of the city, its relation to his own Brooklyn, its geography. His portrait of the stockyards is a microcosmic orgy of Chicago violence that forecasts the future of the convention, and it is a good example of Mailer at his best. It is also inaccurate, as the stockyards are now more modern than he thinks; the operators use tranquilizers on the animals and are a smaller business than they used to be. Many of the facts are wrong, but, as Raymond Mungo would say, the truth is there nonetheless. Mailer captures the spirit of the violence that was brought down on the heads of demonstrators and innocent bystanders in the streets of Chicago, and he portrays the people and their way of life:

> In the slaughterhouse, during the day, a carnage worthy of the Disasters of War took place each morning and afternoon. . . . What an awful odor the fear of absolute and unavoidable death gave to the stool and stuffing and pure vomitous shit of beasts waiting in the pens in the stockyard, what a sweat of hell-leather, and yet the odor, no, the titanic stench, which rose from the yards was not so simple as the collective diarrhetics of an hysterical army of beasts, no, for after the throats were cut and the blood ran in rich gutters, red light on the sweating back of the red throat-cutters, the dying and some just dead animals clanked along the overhead, arterial blood spurting like the nip-ups of a little boy urinating in public, the red-hot carcass quickly encountered another Black or Hunkie with a long knife on a long stick who would cut the belly from the chest to groin and a stew and a stink of two hundred pounds of stomach, lungs, intestines . . . and general gag-all would flop and slither over the floor, the man with the knife getting a good blood-splatting as he dug and twisted with his blade to liberate the roots of the organ, intestine and impedimenta still integrated into the meat and bone of the excavated existence he was working on. . . .
>
> Yes, Chicago was a town where nobody could ever forget how the money was made. It was picked up from floors still slippery with blood. . . . So something of the entrails and the secrets of the gut got into the faces of

native Chicagoans. . . . it was the last of the great American cities, and people had great faces, carnal as blood, greedy, direct, too impatient for hypocrisy, in love with honest plunder. (88-90)

In this renovation of Sandburg, Mailer is suggesting the psychic landscape of the convention and city controlled by Mayor Richard Daley and, at a powerful remove, Lyndon Johnson. As in other passages in this part, Mailer seems more attracted to than repelled by the violence he observes here and condemns later when it is directed against demonstrators as well as reporters and innocent bystanders; and it is this peculiar attraction which allows him to write about it so well, directly and without euphemisms—a journalistic attitude which is tuned to the directness and brutal honesty he associates with the city he describes.

With the appetite of a journalist, Mailer collects the data that he forms into the backdrop of the Chicago drama. Then, with the sensibility and imagination of the novelist, he plays his characters and episodes against that backdrop, which serves as a measuring stick for the people involved, a context and reason for the events. Senator Eugene McCarthy and his followers, for instance, have "thin noses, and thin . . . nostrils" compared to the face of Chicago, which "might be reduced to a broad fleshy nose with nostrils open wide to stench, stink, power, a pretty day, a well-stacked broad, and the beauties of a dirty buck . . . " (90-91). Humphrey, on the other hand, is adapted to the environment: "The Mafia loved Humphrey . . . and there was big money behind Humphrey, . . . in the Hilton called the Hubaret . . . you needed a scorecard to separate the trade-union leaders from the Maf . . ." (110). McGovern, "reminiscent of Henry Fonda" (122), does not blend well. The protestors, violent or Gandhian, are clearly in the land of the enemy. Mayor Daley is clearly in his element, controlling the convention directly from the floor, controlling the streets through hundreds of Chicago-hardened policemen who are also in their element, though many were fearful and maniacal enough to riot under Daley's command.

Mailer is continuously broadening the context of the Chicago convention by drawing in Bobby Kennedy's assassination (as well as his detailed personal reaction), Martin Luther King's, or Valerie Solanas' near-fatal shooting of Andy Warhol.

He spins out the context of American violence until, after the convention and riots, the reader perceives clearly that a good journalist of this country's politics has to embrace and articulate a large and very complex universe of events, with Mayor Daley's jowl as "the soft underbelly of the new American axis" (223). Although Mailer spends much of his time inside the convention hall, witnessing a less physical violence than that in the streets (although it was physical inside as well, as many newsmen will testify), he portrays the street violence as having a meaning central to that of the convention and its country; and he supplements his view from the nineteenth floor of the Conrad Hilton with coverage from the *Village Voice,* as well as the New York *Times* and the Washington *Post,* whose reporters, like all media people, were commonly at odds with the frenzied police and National Guard.

There were two armies in the streets: those who were committed to transforming the convention into a significant turn in recent American history or to destroying it, revealing its brutality and hypocrisy; and those who were committed to crushing dissent, keeping the convention as the seemingly polite meeting of wheeler-dealers, hangers-on, and hack politicians that it largely was, and holding the walls of Daley's fortress. Abbie Hoffman and Allen Ginsberg, yippies and hippies listening to speeches and rock music or yelling "Dump the Hump," "these children like filthy Christians sitting quietly in the grass" (143), the New Left and concerned middle-aged middle-classers, as well as militant or peaceful blacks—all attacked by herds of policemen, each in another situation, perhaps, trying "to solve his violence by blanketing it with a uniform" (174), but in the streets of a frightened convention city "a true criminal force, chaotic, improvisational, undisciplined, and finally—sufficiently aroused—uncontrollable" (175). In contrast to Wolfe, Mailer is implicitly moralistic throughout his account of the convention, particularly in his coverage of the riots where the two armies meet (although, as he admits, his nineteenth-floor view allowed an unreal kind of esthetic detachment):

> The police cut through the crowd one way, then cut through them another. They chased people into the park, ran them down, beat them up; they cut through the intersection at Michigan and Balbo like a razor cutting a chan-

nel through a head of hair, and then drove columns of new police into the channel who in turn pushed out, clubs flailing, on each side, to cut new channels, and new ones again. As demonstrators ran, they reformed in new groups only to be chased by the police again. The action went on for ten minutes, fifteen minutes, with the absolute ferocity of a tropical storm, and watching it from a window on the nineteenth floor, there was something of the detachment of studying a storm at evening through a glass, the light was a lovely gray-blue, the police had uniforms of sky-blue, even the ferocity had an abstract elemental play of forces of nature at battle with other forces, as if sheets of tropical rain were driving across the street in patterns. . . . The reporter . . . could understand now how Mussolini's son-in-law had once been able to find the bombs he dropped from his airplane beautiful as they burst, yes, children, and youths, and middle-aged men and women were being pounded and clubbed and gassed and beaten, hunted and driven, sent scattering in all directions by teams of policemen who had exploded out of their re-straints like the bursting of a boil. . . .

A great stillness rose from the street through all the small noise of clubbing and cries, small sirens, sigh of loaded arrest vans as off they pulled, shouts of police as they wheeled in larger circles, the intersection clearing further, then further, a stillness rose through the steel and stone of the hotel, congregating in the shocked centers of every room where delegates and wives and Press and cam-paign workers innocent until now of the intimate working of social force, looked down now into the murderous para-digm of Vietnam there beneath them at this huge inter-section of this great city. (169-172)

In 1965 Mailer said that novelists were "no longer writing about the beast but, as in the case of Hemingway . . . , about the paw of the beast, or in Faulkner about the dreams of the beast."[9] In *Miami and the Siege of Chicago* he has recorded as a journalist what he created fictionally as a novelist: the move-ments, the actuality, of the beast at the heart of American politics. Even if Mailer is somehow limited psychologically by his posing as a tough-guy intellectual—especially near the end of the book—the reader occasionally put off by his musing on his own cowardice and compromised existence, and the events of Chicago partly transcendent to the imagination of a writer slightly displaced from the present activist generation, who is perhaps ironically better attuned to the slow-paced subtleties of the Miami convention, it is also true that he has written an admirable piece of imaginative personal journalism. The political events of the present demand a tremendous effort of anyone to comprehend, and they involve, as Mailer says, "large thoughts for a reporter to have" (188).

Mailer spent his time after the conventions making movies at his own expense and running in the Democratic primary for mayor of New York City. In the spring of 1969, during the campaign, he was contracted by *Life* to write a book-length series of articles about the U.S. space program. The first installment, "A Fire on the Moon," concerning the Apollo 11 flight, appeared in the 29 August issue. It was following by a second, "The Psychology of Astronauts," written after the Apollo 11 astronauts' return, which appeared 14 November, and a third, "A Dream of the Future's Face," 9 January 1970.[10] Mailer's account is easily the best of its kind I have read. It is a *tour de force* in journalistic writing about contemporary technology, science, and their human and political milieu.[11] I would like to discuss the first two installments, as representative of this work, in some detail, omitting consideration of the third, which, though good, is more speculative than reportorial.

In "A Fire on the Moon," Mailer takes as his starting point the suicide of Ernest Hemingway and construes it as an emblem of the end of a romanticism that survived into an age of dread, now become an age of space technology which must be understood:

> We are obliged after all to comprehend the astronauts. If we approach our subject via Aquarius, it is because he is a detective of sorts, and different in spirit from eight years ago. He has learned to live with questions. Of course, as always, he has little to do with the immediate spirit of the time. Which is why Norman on this occasion may call himself Aquarius. Born January 31, he is entitled to the name, but he thinks it a fine irony that we now enter the Aquarian Period since he has never had less sense of possessing the age. He feels in fact little more than a decent

spirit, somewhat shunted to the side. It is the best possible position for detective work. (25-26)

There is here some of the feeling of Henry Adams, the nineteenth-century man, encountering the dynamo of the twentieth century, as Adams recorded it in his autobiography, *The Education of Henry Adams.* There is additional support for the idea that the events of the Chicago convention may have partly transcended Mailer's imagination; but here, as there, and as in Adams' own case, the displacement, no matter what its extent, is used to the advantage of gaining perspective. Here it places Mailer in the position of a detective, a man who must work through the displacement to articulate the mystery, who will communicate to us a record of his discoveries.

Again he creates a name, "Aquarius," from a third-person point of view, for his protagonist. Again he tries to place himself properly in relation to the narrative that follows: to be *in* enough that the story will be personal and tuned to his own present sensibility, but *out* enough that he will avoid the chains of self-consciousness and the temptation of exhibitionism. With the Democratic primary for mayor over (he having come in fourth out of five), Mailer considers himself superbly ready for the assignment at hand, "For he was detached this season from the imperial demands of his ego; he could think about astronauts, space, space programs, and the moon, quite free of the fact that none of these heroes, presences, and forces were by any necessity friendly to him" (26). Thus prepared, he reflects on his technique as a journalist:

> He preferred to divine an event through his senses—since he was as nearsighted as he was vain, he tended to sniff out the center of a situation from a distance. So his mind often stayed out of contact with the workings of his brain for days at a time. When it was time, lo and behold, he seemed to have comprehended the event. That was one advantage of using the nose—technology had not yet succeeded in elaborating a science of smell. (26)

Mailer, perhaps resolving the Eliotic "dissociation of sensibility," approaches his subject with a kind of childlike sense of wonder and openness—a starting point for any really good journalist—which he tempers with moral judgment and esthetic control derived from experience.

Here, in the world of the space program, he is in new territory, but his senses are open, his mind articulate; and he tends to evaluate and define through an awareness of the people he encounters and through a sixth sense about the political logic of all large American events. In a swamp of technological happenings and terminology Mailer picks up the vibrations of the people. He notices, for instance, the "absolute lack of surface provocation, or idiosyncrasy of personality, which characterizes physicists, engineering students, statisticians, computer technicians, and many a young man of science" (27). Personality is an important key in unlocking the mythology of astronautics. Consider his portrait of Werner von Braun, for instance:

> Yes, Von Braun most definitely was not like other men. Curiously shifty, as if to show his eyes in full would give away too much, a man who wheeled whole complexes of cautions into every gesture—he was after all an engineer who put massive explosives into adjoining tanks and then was obliged to worry about leaks. What is plumbing after all but the prevention of treachery in closed systems? So he would never give anything away he did not have to, but the secrets he held, the tensions he held, the very philosophical explosives he contained under such super-compression gave him an air of magic. He was a rocketeer. . . . Immediate reflection must tell you that a man who wishes to reach heavenly bodies is an agent of the Lord or Mephisto. In fact, Von Braun, with his handsome spoiled face, massive chin, and long and highly articulated nose, had a fair resemblance to Goethe. (Albeit none of the fine weatherings of the Old Master's head.) But brood on it: . . . What went on in Von Braun's mind during a dream? (34)

Mailer, trained in his youth as an engineer, is also at home with much of the technology, although he admits that, like most world citizens of his generation, he is unable to comprehend the whole character of the change it has wrought. The Vehicle Assembly Building he sees as "the first cathedral of the age of technology"—a kind of metaphorical knowledge that distinguishes him as a writer—but "this emergence of a ship to travel the ether, thrust across a vacuum, was no event he could measure by any philosophy he had yet put together in his brain" (30). Nonetheless, his awe at the largeness of the event, combined with his talent as a writer, makes his account of the launching a memorable piece of journalism. He sees the rising ship as a "slim angelic mysterious ship of stages . . . slow as Melville's Leviathan might swim" (40). His final note, however, is moral, for the event is not unambiguously moral—that much of its technological implications Mailer comprehends as he quotes Reverend Abernathy after the launch: "This is really holy ground. And it will be more holy once we feed the hungry, care for the sick, and provide for those who do not have houses" (40).

In the second installment, "The Psychology of Astronauts," Mailer applies himself to the problem of journalistically presenting the astronauts by reporting and analyzing their comments on the technicalities of the flight, by exploring his own complex reactions to the men, and by relating their psychology to the historical context and mythology of the Apollo 11 event. He sees Aldrin as "all meat and stone, . . . a man of solid presentation, dependable as a tractor, but suggesting the strength of a tank, dull, almost ponderous, yet with the hint of unpredictability" (53). Collins, in contrast to Aldrin, "moved easily; Collins was cool. Collins was the man nearly everybody was glad to see at a party, for he was the living spirit of good and graceful manners" (54). Armstrong, however, is an enigma:

> So Armstrong seemed of all the astronauts the man nearest to being saintly, yet there was something as hard, small-town and used in his face as the look of a cashier over pennies. . . . He could be an angel, he could be the town's most unsavory devil. You could not penetrate the flash of the smile—all of America's bounty was in it. Readiness to serve, innocence, competence, modesty, sly humor, and then a lopsided yawning slide of a dumb smile at the gulf of one's own ignorance, like oops am I small-town dumb!— that was also in it. (55)

All three of the astronauts are finally, for Mailer, men who are contradictory in character. What he has learned of them leads to the final commentary:

> It was the most soul-destroying and apocalyptic of centuries. So in their turn the astronauts had personalities of

unequaled banality and apocalyptic dignity. So they suggested in their contradictions the power of the century to live with its own incredible contradictions and yet release some of the untold energies of the earth. A century devoted to the rationality of technique was also a century so irrational as to open in every mind the real possibility of global destruction. . . . As one had only to listen to an astronaut speak for a few minutes to know that his comprehension of unconscious impulses was technical, not carnal, so did the century suggest that its tendency was unconscious of itself. The itch was to accelerate—the metaphysical direction unknown. (63)

To know an age is to know its men. Mailer, as a writer, understands the significance of that idea; and, as a New Journalist, he knows that one writes of the world and its men through one's own reaction to them, whether that reaction be called objective or personal. For Mailer journalism is fundamentally an art, creative and honest, and he has contributed a great deal toward its future development.

I have devoted this chapter to Capote, Wolfe, and Mailer as three major stylists of the New Journalism because I think they fill those roles, at least during the decade of the 1960's with which we are concerned. They defined and pursued new stylistic directions, and they have influenced many other journalists within the last few years. That is not to say that they are absolutely the most important journalists of the 1960's— though in many ways they are—for there are many others who have been influential in changing the style of traditional journalism who are also important and articulate writers, such as John Hersey, whom I mentioned earlier and will turn to again, Jimmy Breslin, Dan Wakefield, and Hunter Thompson—all of whom, along with some journalists of the underground press, I will consider in the next two chapters.

If Robert Scholes is right in his theory, quoted earlier, that the realistic novel or, more generally, realistic fiction is splitting into two new forms, "fabulous non-realistic fiction" and a "creative journalism," then many of the New Journalists, especially those considered in this chapter, are creating a literary genre of the future, as well as recording and assessing an age more richly than has ever been done before. And I would expand his theory to the point of saying that many of the literarily important works of long narrative length in the near future will probably be journalistic, stylistic experiments in the communication of actual events; whereas, on the other hand, much important fiction will be in the form of short, episodic prose pieces, largely fabulous, as he suggests, or fantastic, science-fictional, poetic or hallucinatory, "stoned." (And there may be a subtle significance in the fact that the short prose piece is in some ways a prototypical journalistic form.) Whatever the future, let me turn to some other New Journalists.

4

NEW JOURNALISTS
WRITING ON
THE GENERAL SCENE
AND
THE RACE AND WAR SCENE

This is D. J., Disc Jockey to America turning off. Vietnam, hot dam.

D.J. in Norman Mailer's
Why Are We in Vietnam?

In this and the following chapter I would like to discuss the work of what I hope is an illustrative cross section of New Journalists, besides those dealt with previously. There are many journalists now writing who exemplify certain qualities of style or attitude which I associate with New Journalism; and, taking the term in a broader sense, there are many placing a new emphasis on, and giving a contemporary relevance to, more traditional journalistic kinds of writing. Those of the first type are, at one extreme, creating a new kind of literature, a journalistic art that is significant immediately as well as historically. Hersey's *Hiroshima* (1946) or James Agee's *Let Us Now Praise Famous Men* (1939) come to mind as examples from the pre-1960's, and there are a number of contemporary journalists—besides Capote, Wolfe, and Mailer—like Susan Sontag, James Kunen, and Dan Wakefield, among others, who exemplify the renewal and fruition of this impulse in the last decade. Those of the second type are, at the other extreme, what I call the New Muckrakers. They are not concerned with muckraking, in the popular sense, as exposure for the sake of tabloid reading pleasure or for the purpose of destroying careers; rather, they are, at their best, and like their best predecessors, writing with a clear moral purpose. They are renovating and polishing an old journalistic tool for a new task at hand. Classic examples of such work are Ida M. Tarbell's *History of the Standard Oil Company* (1904) or Upton Sinclair's *The Jungle* (1906)—both of which were books with a moral commitment. Contemporary ones are Joe McGinnis' *The Selling of the President 1968* (1969) and James Ridgeway's *The Closed Corporation* (1968), an exposure of the relations between universities and the military-industrial complex, as well as dozens of others that are of comparable importance.

Ultimately, I think, the New Journalists who are transforming journalism into an art form are the most significant of these two extremes. The work of the New Muckrakers is tremendously significant for the moment, but I don't think it will endure as historically and literarily important as well as the best of the first—though any journalism is subject to the possibility of historical irrelevance. After all, muckraking, even at its best, is primarily a political act rather than an artistic one, although much journalism transcends any literary form it may happen to take. It should be understood, furthermore, that most New Journalists fall somewhere on the spectrum between these two extremes of a personal, creative art and an objective, researched exposure—and most toward the first rather than the second. In the first there are qualities of honesty, vision, and style that are grounded in the person; in the second those qualities are more a product of the facts, the data, and the form they can be given to make an argument, a scientific knowledge, an objective picture. It seems to me that the first, like the confessional style of much contemporary poetry, is more unique to our age and, certainly, more typical of New Journalism as a genre of journalistic writing. However, the writers at these extremes, as well as those along the spectrum in between, all share a strong commitment to the effective communication of informative and honest statements about the contemporary human situation.

Most of the New Journalists of the first type fall into two broad categories with regard to their careers as journalists: either they are journalists who try to develop a new style (Wolfe and Hersey, also a novelist, are examples); or they come to journalistic writing, with a sense of urgency about its importance, as writers in other genres or fields of interest (Mailer and Capote are examples) or as people, usually young, who are not professional writers, who are attracted to it as a means of articulating their experience and of giving a voice to those sharing their world-view and life-style (James Kunen is an example). By way of introducing the writers who follow, I would like to consider briefly two who clearly exemplify these two categories: Jimmy Breslin and Susan Sontag.

Jimmy Breslin was a relatively unknown sportswriter in 1963 when he was hired as a columnist by the New York *Herald Tribune*. During the years before the *Tribune's* merger with the *World Telegram and Sun* and the *Journal-American*, he developed one of the most distinctive and vital writing styles in American journalism. He is now regarded by many as part of the modern tradition of journalism which includes such writers as Ring Lardner, Ernest Hemingway, and Damon Runyon. He is also one of the forces active in the development of New Journalism. His writing, like Wolfe's, brought a new freshness and dynamism to the *Tribune*, and it suggested the possibilities of future journalism as a literature, an artistic genre, as well as becoming part of and helping to define that genre. Breslin is a professional newspaperman and reporter who goes about his task professionally, and his writing, particularly that about New York, reflects his sense of that role. However, he transforms that role as he lives it, and his writing generally reflects also a personal involvement with and sensitivity to events—qualities which shape his fluid style, like that of Mailer and Wolfe, into a refined resonance with the experiences he reports.

Although Breslin has covered a wide variety of events in his traveling and writing, and written about them well, his coverage of Vietnam is especially good and exemplifies very clearly the style of his journalism. Consider, for example, these commentarial vignettes of the war:

> George Sunderland rolled over on his cot in the hut and his foot caught the mosquito netting and pulled part of it onto the bed. Mosquito netting should hang straight, from the rod on the ceiling over the cot down to the floor, so that the rat crawling up it follows the netting to the ceiling and does not get a grip on the cot with its feet. Sunderland's foot made a fold in the netting and the rat crawling up it came into the fold and onto the bed. The rat's small mouth moved and its teeth came through the netting and into Sunderland's foot. Sunderland kicked the rat and the rat fell under the cot. The rat crept away with its tail dragging across the dirt floor. . . .

Viet Nam, which is a little war of rats, is like this always. It is a place of sneaking and gnawing and of people who see nothing and hear nothing and spend days finding nothing, and who are hit in the back by a shot that comes from nowhere. Nothing seems to happen, and then a Marine battalion is sent home after seven months and it has not been in one action and it has 10 percent casualties.

It is a place where people are hurt and die in little situations, and very little is heard of it because it is all so scattered. But it is here.

The big-bladed fan in the ceiling spun slowly over Richard Nixon's head while he sat on a couch Saturday night and said he thought the military part of the war could go on for two or three more years.[1]

Breslin has a storyteller's sense of irony and an awareness of the revelations inherent in details. He has caught the physical and moral character of Vietnam in a perfect conjunction, and we see that conjunction through the sensibility of a writer who is deeply concerned about what he is reporting. The narrative is accurate and moving, and there is an artistry in the style, though it is in a lower key than that of Mailer, perhaps closer to Joseph Heller or Kurt Vonnegut. It is a far more imaginative and personally relevant kind of journalism than one can find in most newspapers.

Before 1968, Susan Sontag was well known as a perceptive critic, essayist, and novelist, and as a regular contributor to such journals as *Partisan Review*. With her account of a 1968 trip to North Vietnam, *Trip to Hanoi*, published in *Esquire*, December 1968, she emerged as a good and potentially important and influential New Journalist.[2] Her conversion to journalistic writing is a textbook case:

Though I have been and am passionately opposed to the American aggression in Vietnam, I accepted the unexpected invitation to go to Hanoi that came in mid-April with the pretty firm idea that I wouldn't write about the trip upon my return. Being neither a journalist nor a political activist (though a veteran signer of petitions and antiwar demonstrator) nor an Asian specialist, but rather a stubbornly unspecialized writer who has so far been largely unable to incorporate into either novels or essays my evolving radical political convictions and sense of moral dilemma at being a citizen of the American empire, I doubted that my account of such a trip could add anything new to the already eloquent opposition to the war. And contributing to the anti-war polemic seemed to me the only worthwhile reason for an American to be writing about Vietnam now.

Perhaps the difficulty started there, with the lack of a purpose that really justified in my own mind my being invited to North Vietnam. Had I brought some clear intentions about the usefulness (to me or to anyone else) of my visit, I probably would have found it easier to sort out and assimilate what I saw. If occasionally I could have reminded myself that I was a writer and Vietnam was "material," I might have fended off some of the confusions that beset me. As it was, the first days of my stay were profoundly discouraging, with most of my energies going toward trying to keep my gloom within tolerable limits. But now that I'm back, and since returning want after all to write about North Vietnam, I don't regret that early decision. By denying myself a role that could have shielded me from my ignorance and spared me a lot of personal discomfort, I unwittingly assisted what discoveries I eventually made during the trip.[3]

Thus, like many New Journalists, she came to her task without any preconceptions about her role or about how she would write, and her style finally emerged as closely correlated with the character of her experience in North Vietnam. It is interesting to note that her account of being open, intentionally or not, to a new experience as a means of journalistically tuning-in to it is similar to Mailer's in "A Fire on the Moon." Both of them, like Wolfe and many other New Journalists, exemplify this trait of a creative openness which is one of the prerequisites of the best New Journalistic writing.

What Sontag hints at in this opening passage is the idea of a change of consciousness, a transformation in the nature of her awareness of North Vietnam and the relentless allegiance of its people, as a necessity for writing about them properly. Her account is primarily about this change of consciousness, about the effect it had on her as a person, on her understanding of the revolution-minded North Vietnamese, and on the way in which she would write the account. She speaks of her prior knowledge of North Vietnam as consisting of "images" from books and the media. They don't suffice to prepare her for the experience of the trip:

> the confrontation with the originals of these images didn't prove to be a simple experience; actually to see and touch them produced an effect both exhilarating and numbing. Matching concrete reality with mental image was at best a mechanical or merely additive process, while prying new facets from the Vietnamese officials and ordinary citizens I was meeting was a task for which I'm not particularly well equipped. Unless I could effect in myself some changes of awareness, of consciousness, it would scarcely matter that I'd actually been to Vietnam. But that was exactly what was so hard, since I had only my own culture-bound, disoriented sensibility for an instrument. (209)

In reading the dated pages of Sontag's journal, one can see that she did succeed in effecting this change, to a remarkable extent; and it is certainly that change, in large part, which makes the book an outstanding documentary of her personal encounter with the country, as well as a valuable example of New Journalistic writing.

The alteration of her awareness allowed Sontag to transcend the images of the media and her own cultural preconceptions to such an extent that she is able to offer many sympathetic and insightful statements about the character of the North Vietnamese people and their view of the war. Those statements are derived from a personal struggle for understanding, but they have, finally, a weight of anthropological truth and objectivity. Here are a few:

> They live exclusively in the world of history. (219)

> This is history for use—for survival, to be precise—and it is an entirely *felt* history, not the preserve of detached intellectual concern. (220)

> The principle of total use [efficient use of all matériel, scrap included] applies not only to things but to thoughts as well. . . . As each material object must be made to go a long way, so must each idea. Vietnamese leaders specialize in an economical, laconic wisdom. (255)

I found, through direct experience, North Vietnam to be a place which, in many respects, *deserves* to be idealized. (259)

. . . in the end, of course, an American has no way of incorporating Vietnam into his consciousness. (271)

Sontag invites the reader to share with her the lived truth of Hegel's maxim that "the problem of history is the problem of consciousness" and to emerge with a new knowledge of the North Vietnamese people. From her observations of other facets of their lives, it becomes clear that the American mentality is alienated considerably from their way of experiencing the world. She suggests as a partial overcoming of this problem that North Vietnam be conceived of as a country in permanent revolution, much as America was two hundred years ago, as a country engaged in a struggle for a politics of humanity—regardless of the clichés established through news reports and the rhetoric of either the North Vietnamese or the American government. She herself has done admirably well in the attempt to see the North Vietnamese with new eyes, as her day-to-day record of the stay shows, and she has communicated with great articulateness her personal involvement in that attempt. Her effort is exemplary of those of many New Journalists who recognize the need for new reportorial forms and techniques, and for whom a new awareness of human reality is not only the reason for, but also a product of, the New Journalism.

THE GENERAL SCENE

One of the best book-length New Journalistic works of general interest is Dan Wakefield's *Supernation at Peace and War*. Wakefield is a talented journalistic writer who has written a number of other good journalistic books and, recently, a novel, *Going All the Way*. He wrote *Supernation at Peace and War* after four months of traveling through the ghettos, suburbs, small towns, and countrysides of most of the United States and, briefly, Canada. The book is one man's report of what was happening in America in 1967 and 1968. He tries to convey a sense of the life-styles and preoccupations of widely varied groups of people, but—a very telling fact about the

American devotion to "scientific" modes of activity—he was held in suspicion by many because his work was not subject to the control and scrutiny of computers and research teams. His personal report involves a transcendence of the usual bureaucratic news-gathering apparatus, and it is one of the most useful and enlightening journalistic works of the last few years.

Wakefield, like Wolfe, is concerned with the way in which conventional journalism presents important and revealing aspects of American culture as not mattering. Concerning the "spring mobilization for peace" marches, consisting of about a quarter of a million people in New York City and 60,000 in San Francisco, Wakefield notes:

> *Time* magazine, an invaluable publication for revealing what is socially and politically acceptable in the society at any given time, said that the main thing that the demonstrations showed was that "Americans in the springtime like to have fun."
>
> Since at a minimum estimate well over 100,000 people participated in the demonstration [in New York], there was no way to deny that it happened. But that was not the important thing.
>
> *The important thing was that it didn't count. . . .*
>
> The *Time* magazine coverage of the demonstration was accompanied by seven photographs. The photographs showed (1) a crowd of youths gathered around a Russian flag and an upside-down American flag; (2) a pair of American Indians; (3) some long-haired boys burning draft cards; (4) Drs. King and Spock, the co-leaders of the march in New York; (5) a hippie with a tambourine around his neck; (6) a hippie girl with a banana around her neck; (7) a hippie girl with "Peace" painted under one eye. Under the three photos of the hippies was a caption which said, "Speaking eloquently for what the U.S. is trying to defend," leaving any literal-minded reader with the notion that the U.S. has a million troops stationed around the world in order to defend the rights of people everywhere to wear tambourines and bananas around their necks.
>
> At any rate, one could obviously see by looking at the pictures that this was a bunch of kooks and possibly some Communists. . . . The text of the story did not

mention much other participation except for noting the presence of students from Smith and Vassar and some "Columbia University scholars," which hardly changed the overall picture for the average middle-class American reader. . . . No doubt many people in the march were rather discouraged when they got home and found that they had all been transformed into exotic long-haired hippies through the magic of modern journalism.[4]

Wakefield, who was present at the New York demonstration, makes it clear that there was a much larger variety of people present, including veterans and women from various organizations; and he wrote his book partly as a corrective for this kind of conventional journalism and its unjust coverage.

Wakefield is concerned with his report as a way of transcending or at least clarifying the "credibility gap" that exists between the people and the government by offering an honest, personal, and yet factually objective impression of the American situation—at least as seen by one intelligent and morally involved reporter. He is trying to use his own journalism as a way of overcoming "the information glut," a phenomenon related to the "credibility gap" and to what Lazarsfeld and Merton, in my first chapter, termed the "narcotizing dysfunction" of the media. It is, according to Wakefield,

a by-product of mass communications which does not produce informed support or protest on any given issue but rather leads to the silence of confusion and resignation. The cross fire of charges and denials on a subject as controversial as the war, the contradictory "facts" reported by experts and on-the-spot observers, the daily onslaught of "news" about the war lead many educated people to throw up their hands and forget about it rather than attempt to sort out what they should believe and how they should feel from the hundreds of columns, books, news stories, television clips, radio broadcasts, Congressional debates, academic teach-ins, and military and political analyses published and broadcast and rehashed and criticized. (123-124)

Overcoming the "information glut" and making minority events "matter" constitute two major purposes of his book, as they do of the underground press and the writing of many New Journalists. Wakefield, I think, goes an admirably long way toward accomplishing both.

Two other talented New Journalists of the general scene are Studs (Louis) Terkel, a Chicago radioman, and Joan Didion, a Los Angeles novelist-journalist. Terkel's *Division Street: America* (New York: Pantheon Publishers, 1967) and *Hard Times: An Oral History of the Great Depression* (New York: Pantheon Publishers, 1970) are both, like Wakefield's book, attempts at interpreting the *Zeitgeist* by a journalistic survey of popular moods and opinions, except that Terkel presents his material more through the voices of the people he encounters than through his own. *Division Street* consists of dozens of carefully edited and effectively arranged monologues spoken by Chicagoans—young, old, rich, poor, and so forth— concerning their life-styles, their city, the war in Vietnam, poverty, despair, and the other nagging preoccupations of contemporary man. Terkel's ability to distinguish significant and telling human attitudes makes the book a valuable treasury of American moods during the 1960's. *Hard Times* is more specific with regard to subject matter and more general with regard to geography than *Division Street*. In this book Terkel, again armed with his tape recorder and editorial sensitivity, travels across America and compiles a long documentary of the various manifestations of the psychological wound of the Great Depression. The book demonstrates dramatically the gap that exists between the survivors of the depression, who are still bracing themselves protectively against a recurrence through a neurotic quest for total financial security, and their children, who have never experienced such a disaster and are therefore largely indifferent or in opposition to their parents' money-oriented life-style. It is a valuable journalistic study of a historical event which is, if sometimes subtly, still very much alive in American society. Both books, like those of Oscar Lewis, are remarkable records of the concrete realities of the contemporary American character—they are a sort of journalistic *cinéma vérité*—and are as useful for the sociologist as they are educational for the reading public.

Joan Didion's *Slouching Towards Bethlehem,* a collection of her best nonfiction writing from several magazines—including, oddly enough, the *Saturday Evening Post*—is one of the most engaging, well-written, and sensitive works of New Journalism published to date. The title is taken from William Butler Yeats' poem "The Second Coming" and refers to the fragmentation and disorder of the contemporary world where "the center cannot hold" and yet where some new but still uncertain order may be emerging. It is thus the historically transitional and apocalyptic aspect of events which attracts her attention; she is very much involved in what she discerns, and records it with relentless honesty and a poetic or prophetic awareness of its meaning.

Like Wakefield's book, *Slouching Towards Bethlehem* is about several parts of America and about a variety of different kinds of people. There are vignettes on Newport ("The Seacoast of Despair") and Alcatraz Island ("Rock of Ages") as well as longer pieces on Hawaii ("Letter from Paradise, 20° 19′ N., 157° 52′ W.") and New York ("Goodbye to All That"). "Marrying Absurd," a short piece about Las Vegas marriages, is reminiscent of Wolfe's writing about the same place; and "Slouching Towards Bethlehem," the title piece and the longest of the collection, is an intriguing and often ironic journal of Didion's experiences in Haight-Ashbury just before its dissolution and shows her to be as skeptical of its morality and future as Nicholas von Hoffman is in his book *We Are the People Our Parents Warned Us Against*, which I will discuss in the next chapter.

A good example of Didion's writing about place is "Some Dreamers of the Golden Dream," which is about the San Bernardino Valley, its people, and the stories surrounding Lucille Miller's conviction of murdering her husband, Cork. The piece might be described as a sort of article-length *In Cold Blood*, save that it is concerned with more ambiguous events and a region very different from western Kansas, and Didion reminds one of Capote in her creation of a suspenseful consciousness of place:

> This is a story about love and death in the golden land, and begins with the country. The San Bernardino Valley lies only an hour east of Los Angeles by the San Bernardino Freeway but is in certain ways an alien place: not the coastal California of the subtropical twilights and the soft westerlies off the Pacific but a harsher California, haunted by the Mojave just beyond the mountains, devastated by the hot dry Santa Ana wind that comes down

through the passes at 100 miles an hour and whines through the eucalyptus windbreaks and works on the nerves. October is the bad month for the wind, the month when breathing is difficult and the hills blaze up spontaneously. There has been no rain since April. Every voice seems a scream. It is the season of suicide and divorce and prickly dread, wherever the wind blows.

The Mormons settled this ominous country, and then they abandoned it, but by the time they left the first orange tree had been planted and for the next hundred years the San Bernardino Valley would draw a kind of people who imagined they might live among the talismanic fruit and prosper in the dry air, people who brought with them Midwestern ways of building and cooking and praying and who tried to graft those ways upon the land. The graft took in curious ways. This is the California where it is possible to live and die without ever eating an artichoke, without ever meeting a Catholic or a Jew. This is the California where it is easy to Dial-A-Devotion, but hard to buy a book. This is the country in which a belief in the literal interpretation of Genesis has slipped imperceptibly into a belief in the literal interpretation of *Double Indemnity,* the country of the teased hair and the Capris and the girls for whom all life's promise comes down to a waltz-length white wedding dress and the birth of a Kimberly or a Sherry or a Debbi and a Tijuana divorce and a return to hairdressers' school. "We were just crazy kids," they say without regret, and look to the future. The future always looks good in the golden land, because no one remembers the past. Here is where the hot wind blows and the old ways do not seem relevant, where the divorce rate is double the national average and where one person in every thirty-eight lives in a trailer. Here is the last stop for all those who come from somewhere else, for all those who drifted away from the cold and the past and the old ways. Here is where they are trying to find a new life style, trying to find it in the only places they know where to look: the movies and the newspapers. The case of Lucille Marie Maxwell Miller is a tabloid monument to that new life style.[5]

This description of setting is a thoroughly effective introduction to the story which follows. Like Wolfe, Didion has the ability to detect and bring to life through description and suggestion the near-explosive madness and emptiness beneath the surface of patterns of living usually regarded as normative and typically American.

Didion is attracted by a number of intriguing personalities, especially John Wayne ("John Wayne: A Love Song"), the Communist Michael Laski ("Comrade Laski, C.P.U.S.A., [M.-L.]"), and Howard Hughes ("7000 Romaine, Los Angeles 38"). The piece on Hughes is particularly interesting because in it one sees her more philosophical and speculative power of mind in action as she considers the mythical significance of a man who is himself a modern myth. She, like Mailer, is an astute, journalistic interpreter of the relations between personalities and history:

> Our favorite people and our favorite stories become so not by any inherent virtue, but because they illustrate something deep in the grain, something unadmitted. Shoeless Joe Jackson, Warren Gamaliel Harding, the *Titantic: how the mighty are fallen.* Charles Lindbergh, Scott and Zelda Fitzgerald, Marilyn Monroe: *the beautiful and the damned.* And Howard Hughes. That we have made a hero of Howard Hughes tells us something interesting about ourselves, something only dimly remembered, tells us that the secret point of money and power in America is neither the things that money can buy nor power for power's sake (Americans are uneasy with their possessions, guilty about power, all of which is difficult for Europeans to perceive because they are themselves so truly materialistic, so versed in the uses of power), but absolute personal freedom, mobility, privacy. It is the instinct which drove America to the Pacific, all through the nineteenth century, the desire to be able to find a restaurant open in case you want a sandwich [a reason she was told why Hughes is buying up Las Vegas], to be a free agent, live by one's own rules. . . . It is impossible to think of Howard Hughes without seeing the apparently bottomless gulf between what we say we want and what we do want, between what we officially admire and secretly desire, between, in the largest sense, the people we marry and the people we love. In a nation which increasingly appears to prize social virtues, Howard Hughes remains not merely antisocial but

grandly, brilliantly, surpassingly, asocial. He is the last private man, the dream we no longer admit. (71, 72)

This analytical mood extends to other topical pieces, such as "On Self-Respect" and "On Morality," and to those that are more personal, such as "On Going Home" and "On Keeping a Notebook." In the last Didion discusses her habit of keeping a notebook and thereby discloses a good deal about her character as a journalist:

> Keepers of private notebooks are a different breed altogether, lonely and resistant rearrangers of things, anxious malcontents, children afflicted apparently at birth with some presentiment of loss. . . . I imagine . . . that the notebook is about other people. But of course it is not. . . . My stake is always, of course, in the unmentioned girl in the plaid silk dress. *Remember what it was to be me:* that is always the point. . . . however dutifully we record what we see around us, the common denominator of all we see is always, transparently, shamelessly, the implacable "I." (132-33, 135, 136)

Like most New Journalists, Didion is aware of her personal involvement in the events, situations, and personalities about which she writes; she is honest about that involvement and knows that it can lead her into irrelevant sentimentality or into a richly creative journalism. Her book is an example of the triumph of the latter. Her book is also a way, for her and for the reader, of coming to terms with disorder, a problem she discusses in her preface and alludes to again in the passages quoted above when she speaks of "some presentiment of loss." Her book is finally, like almost all New Journalism in an age when in many ways "Mere anarchy is loosed upon the world," not only a way of coming to terms with disorder but also an attempt, through articulate journalism, to suggest the tenuous patterns of a new order, or a recovery of the best of the old, which is hopefully coming about.

Another book of general interest is Harlan Ellison's *The Glass Teat,* a collection of pieces from his column of the same name for the Los Angeles *Free Press.* The book is subtitled *Essays of Opinion on the Subject of Television* (mostly written during 1969), although, as Ellison says, he is not *really* talking about television but about "dissidence, repression, censorship, the brutality and stupidity of much of our culture, the threat of the Common Man, the dangers of being passive in a time when the individual is merely cannon-fodder, the lying and cheating and killing our 'patriots' do in the sweet name of the American Way."[6] It is, in short, a collection of television reviews with digressions written for a newspaper of the underground press, which Ellison regards as "the last bastion of genuinely free journalistic speech in America" (10). Ellison is a screenplay and science-fiction writer of enormous output who comes to journalism fresh, energetic, and willing to spill everything he regards as significant. Although he is limited as a stylist, he is an imaginative and prolific writer who is morally committed to what he says.

Besides his critically insightful observations about television programming, its banality and ambiguous morality, as well as about the media and their country in general, he offers an account of a "two-day lecture/lynching" at the Dayton Living Arts Center in Dayton, Ohio, which concludes the collection and is a good minor example of the kind of personal reportage associated with New Journalism. Ellison was invited to the Center to speak to various groups about his work as a writer, but he went further, to the extent of describing the nature of his commitment as a writer in a sick society, and wound up being dismissed by Glenn Ray and the Center's administration as too radical. He had, according to his own report, reached the people he spoke to, particularly a class of black students, in a way they had never been reached before. He describes his dismissal as

> A wound neither as deep as a Chicago Conspiracy Trial nor as wide as two US Army sergeants being removed from their Armed Forces Radio posts when they told their audience that they were being censored and could not tell the troops what was *really* happening in the War. Neither as final as the silencing of Lenny Bruce . . . nor as significant as the attempted whitewash of My Lai before the evidence piled up so high it *couldn't* be denied (though *Time* reported last week that 54% of the American people *still* refuse to believe it happened); . . . neither as debilitating as canceling Joyce Miller's *Encounter* from KPFK because she was sniping at the Administration . . . nor as horrendous as the Smothers Brothers being flushed

out of sight; . . . nor as ghastly as court-martialing soldiers who protest. But Glenn Ray panicked at the two or three phone calls he'd gotten from parents who didn't want their kids to hear any opinions but ones approved by the *Good Housekeeping* seal . . . when he grew terrified that his petty sinecure at the Center was in danger . . . the poison . . . took effect, and he canceled me out. (301-2)

This passage is of special interest because it dramatizes the intimacy of Ellison's beliefs about the need for freedom of speech, especially of a journalistic kind, and his own life as a writer. He cannot be classified as a leftist or a hippie or even as a member of the underground press, since he doesn't belong to the staff of the *Free Press*. He is a unique kind of individualist, and his writing reflects that fact. As a television critic, he is intelligently open to the possibilities of programming and is as willing to recognize the value of *Laugh-In* or *First Tuesday* as he is to condemn such inanities as *Gomer Pyle*. He has, indeed, created the kind of freewheeling and meaningful TV-commentary journalism that has been needed for two decades. Clearly, his writing requires a sense of freedom, and that writing itself is a critique of the limits of freedom of expression in the media and in the country at large. It is freedom and a variety of individualisms, as well as literary talent and a sense of urgency, that have made the New Journalism possible. That it has succeeded as much as it has is a tribute to writers like Ellison and the journalists of the underground who challenge the lip-service paid to real freedom of speech by the governments of this country.

THE RACE AND WAR SCENE

There are many good journalistic books, published during the 1960's, concerning a specific group or event that is of general social or political importance. There are three I would like to discuss in the order of their publication: Jonathan Kozol's *Death at an Early Age*, John Hersey's *The Algiers Motel Incident*, and Gene Marine's *The Black Panthers*. I would also add a fourth, published in 1970 but concerning an event of the late 1960's, Seymour M. Hersh's *My Lai 4*, which, with the three above, completes a kind of journalistic tetralogy dealing with American racism and militance in both domestic and foreign contexts. These books also represent four different kinds of reportage practiced by New Journalists: Kozol's book is a personal account of his experience as a teacher in a black ghetto school in Boston; Hersey's is a collection of vignettes, episodes, testimonies, short interviews, and fragmentary accounts gathered during his visit to Detroit after the riots and the Algiers Motel murders in July 1967; Marine's is an attempt, through personal involvement, interviews, and research, to write an honest and accurate account of the activities of the Black Panthers from their beginning; and Hersh's is, according to its subtitle, *A Report on the Massacre and Its Aftermath,* which is based almost entirely on interviews with military officials and the soldiers of the company involved in the massacre.

Although there are now, unlike five years ago, a number of good books dealing with ghetto schools, Kozol's is still one of the best, and it is representatively New Journalistic.[7] The book was serialized in the Boston *Globe* during October 1967, and parts of it appeared in the *Atlantic,* the *Progressive,* and the *Harvard Educational Review.* The subtitle, *The Destruction of the Hearts and Minds of Negro Children in the Boston Public Schools,* states its subject pretty clearly and suggests that Kozol, like the other three journalists listed above, is a reformist writer, what I earlier termed a New Muckraker. In many ways he is, for, like the other three, he is committed to the exposure of the injustice and inequities inherent in the attitudes and actions of people in a supposedly free society. He differs from them, however, in his being more personally involved in his narrative than they and in his not being originally a journalist, which they all are.

Kozol's book began, he says in the foreword, when he was teaching "in a segregated classroom of the Boston Public Schools" during the 1964-65 academic year:

> With no training in education and no experience as a teacher, I was sent into an overcrowded ghetto school on a substitute basis, given a year-long assignment, though on a day-to-day salary, to teach a Fourth Grade class within a compensatory program that had been designed for Negro children and that was intended to preserve the racial status quo in Boston by upgrading the segregated schools.

Disheartened by conditions in my school building, and being an habitual note-taker, I soon began to amass a large number of envelopes of handwritten notes. By habit, I held onto these notes and, on a free weekend during the middle of the winter, I made a first attempt at putting them together into some sort of shape and sequence. The first outgrowth of this effort was an essay of about thirty-five pages, which I wrote for my own sense of relief and clarification and then set aside, feeling that it had already served its purpose and thinking it of no further use.

In March, however, I showed this writing to a friend of mine, Faith Morrow, who suggested that the essay seemed to her the beginning of a book. I did not think of it again, but continued making jottings and putting them in order and then, at some point in the early summer, after the unexpected events which will be described here had subsided, I began for the first time to see the overall outline of this book.[8]

Like Susan Sontag in her writing of *Trip to Hanoi*, Kozol originally had no intention of writing a book, and that, as in the case of Sontag too, probably helped him to avoid preconceptions about how he would organize the narrative. Consequently, he experienced the year very openly and then gave it a selective reportorial ordering, whereas a journalist might have entered the situation with a knowledge that he would write about it in some fashion—and that fact would undoubtedly have caused him to be selective before Kozol was. The unintentional approach of Kozol and Sontag was surely helpful in allowing them to stay close to their experiences, and that approach is typical of many of the New Journalists in the second category, those who come to journalism from another field of interest.

Kozol's account is full of moderation, modesty, sensitive gentle-mindedness, and intelligence. In a very simple, direct style he presents the story of the ghetto schools, their politically controlled shabby condition, his experience with the students he taught, and his eventual dismissal by the school board for improvising too much on the standard list of reading materials. According to Kozol, that reading list was boring, racially ignorant, and irrelevant to the lives of his students. So he introduced a poem by W. B. Yeats, "The Lake Isle of Innisfree";

several poems by Langston Hughes, a black poet; as well as some paintings by Joan Miro and Paul Klee—which "revolutionary" actions led to his dismissal. The material he introduced brought the grade-school black students to life in a way that none of his other attempts had. As the students were allowed to read only innocuous works by white authors, his reading of Hughes' poems had an especially striking effect.

Kozol recalls that when he was sent to "the highly explosive Patrick Campbell Junior High" to teach eighth-grade children, there was a poem by Edgar Guest on the blackboard:

> One girl read it and then another, and perhaps a few others, and I thought that I had seldom heard anything so hollow and so empty and so redolent of boredom in my life. I asked the children what the poem was about, and none could say. Neither, honestly, in any important sense could I. It was obvious that for these Negro girls—dead-end students already in a dreadful, gloomy, tenth-rate junior high—the idea of poetry, when it meant anything at all, had something to do with big words that you could say in a singsong, recite to show you are a good girl, and do not even attempt to understand. The possibility of its having anything at all to do with your own life or sufferings, or with your own joys and exaltations, was not even in the picture.
>
> That morning in the junior high school I read to the girls in that classroom about half a dozen poems by the Negro poet Langston Hughes. When I held up the book and they saw its new cover, that alone was appealing, for very few new and crisp and fresh-looking volumes ever got in to desecrate those rooms. On the cover they saw the picture of a Negro author, and they commented on that. Their comments had to do with a single, obvious, overriding fact:
>
> *"Look—that man's colored."*
>
> I made a tape-recording of part of my morning in that class. No transistor radios reappeared or were turned on during that next hour and, although some of the children interrupted me a lot to quiz me about Langston Hughes, where he was born, whether he was rich, whether he was married, and about poetry, and about writers, and writing in general, and a number of other things that struck their

fancy, and although it was not a calm or orderly or, above all, disciplined class by traditional definition and there were probably very few minutes in which you would have been able to hear a pin drop or hear my reading uninterrupted by the voices of one or another of the girls, at least I did have their attention and they seemed, if anything, to care only too much about the content of that Negro poet's book. . . . All of them remember the green book of poetry that I read with them that day and, while most of them forget the name of the man who wrote the poetry, they remember the names of the poems he wrote, and they remember something else. They remember that he was Negro. (177-78)

Kozol is not remarkable as a literary stylist, in the way that Mailer is, for instance; but he is a remarkably sensitive observer and has the ability to dramatize well by shifting the pace of his writing and by bringing significant gestures and attitudes to the foreground, and his personalistic point of view keeps the reader almost as close to the experience as he himself was. His story, supplemented by other material in an appendix, is a moving and effective indictment of racism in at least one school system.

Hersey's book, *The Algiers Motel Incident,* is very different from Kozol's. It is more "objective," at least to the extent that it is told in many voices, and it is not so much a story in the narrative sense as it is a pastiche, a collage pieced together toward the solution of a puzzle. Hersey only enters the book as a self-conscious narrator at one point. After a long chart of the people involved in the incident, a Detroit *Free Press* map of the Algiers Motel Annex where the three black men were killed, and some background material, partly from the victims' relations, he removes the reportorial mask to comment upon himself and his task:

At this point in the narrative, enter myself. Reluctantly, I have always, before this, stayed out of my journalism, even as a manipulative pronoun, having believed that it sufficed for a writer to "come through" to the reader—by the nature of his selections from the whole, his filtering of all that had gone through his eyes and ears and mind; by the intensity of feeling that might be read in the lines; by his "voice."

But this account is too urgent, too complex, too dangerous to too many people to be told in a way that might leave doubts strewn along its path; I cannot afford, this time, the luxury of invisibility. For the uses of invisibility, as Ralph Ellison has made so vividly and painfully clear—an inability or unwillingness to see the particularity of one's fellow man, and with it a crucial indifference as to whether one is seen truly as oneself—these uses of not-seeing and not-being-seen are of the essence of racism.[9]

Hersey's intrusion is significant, not only as a device for emphasizing the implications of the events he is reporting through his documents, but also as an act which indicates the New Journalistic character of his writing. He wants the reader to understand that his reportage is no ordinary conventional journalism but one which derives, in spite of its seeming diffusion among many voices, from the moral conviction of its author. This account is no impersonal, neutral, faceless collection of verbiage from a commission or a television "special": it is the work of one man committed to assessing the truth of a multiple murder by an experimental journalistic method. Hersey's experience of gathering information was a startling education, and his account comes through to the reader with the rawness and freshness of that experience.

In August 1967 Hersey had been asked by David Ginsburg, who was the executive director of the President's Commission on Civil Disorders, to write part of the Commission's report. He declined but then came to feel that he owed a debt to the fearful and relentless issue of racial violence; he broke off writing a novel and went to Detroit:

> As I explored Detroit's riot in those first weeks, the incident at the Algiers Motel kept insisting upon attention, and eventually I determined to focus on it. This episode contained all the mythic themes of racial strife in the United States: the arm of the law taking the law into its own hands; interracial sex; the subtle poison of racist thinking by "decent" men who deny that they are racists; the societal limbo into which, ever since slavery, so many young black men have been driven in our country; ambiguous justice in the courts; and the devastation in both black and white human lives that follows in the wake of

violence as surely as ruinous and indiscriminate flood after torrents. (25)

So, with the help of a young woman, Hersey got to know his way around the ghetto and was able, largely on his own, to reach many of the people directly or indirectly involved in the riot and the motel incident. Then there was the problem of how to write about what he learned:

> There was a need, above all, for total conviction. This meant that the events could not be described as if witnessed from above by an all-seeing eye opening on an all-knowing novelistic mind; the merest suspicion that anything had been altered, or made up, for art's sake, or for the sake of effect, would be absolutely disastrous. There could be no "creative reconstruction." Doubts about chronology could only be revealed, not resolved. No names could be changed, because when you change a man's name you change the whole man. The story would have to be told as much as possible in the words of the participants. . . .
>
> Let not any of this suggest to you that I have been trying to persuade you, in the fraudulent tradition of American journalism, that I have been, or shall be, "objective." There is no such thing as an objective reportage. Human life is far too trembling-swift to be reported in the whole; the moment the recorder chooses nine facts out of ten he colors the information with his views. I trust this chapter will have revealed some of my bias for discount.
>
> There were limitations within which I had to work. Trials of this case were being prepared, and some participants could not, and some would not, openly speak to me. I was unable to see three important witnesses. Nevertheless, I think you will find that a great deal was disclosed by those who did talk to me and did testify, for their very speech—the cadences, the images, the texture of the telling, the conscious and the unconscious subterfuges they used—was, in my view, profoundly revealing. (28)

Hersey's account, as he says several times, is necessarily incomplete and, being written before the trials were finished, might distort the legal process; but, he says, he felt a tremendous urgency about the finishing of his book in order in some way to promote interracial "health." He was motivated by a belief "that every scrap of understanding, every door-crack glimmer of illumination, every thread that may lead not just to survival of the races but to health—all should be shared as soon as possible. There is so much to be done in so little time" (28). And it is relevant to note that he says "I will not take any money from any source for publication of this story" (28). His honesty and conviction are apparent throughout the narrative, and he has taken pains to fill out the whole story as fully as possible. He wants, as he says, "understanding," and it is that desire primarily which caused him to avoid the novel-istic form of Capote's *In Cold Blood* or his own earlier *Hiroshima*. Both of those books dealt with events which, in a sense, had already occurred or were capable of being seen historically, whereas domestic racial violence is more obviously continuous into the present moment—and that fact prompted the New Journalistic shift in the kind of reportage he considered relevant and moving.

Gene Marine's book, *The Black Panthers*, is neither consistently personal, like Kozol's book—though Marine is occasionally present in events or interviews—nor is it an experimental documentary like Hersey's. It is basically an extended analytical and explanatory account of the Black Panthers; and it is a very honest book, one in which the writer's beliefs, prejudices, and fears are kept "up front," so that the reader knows where he stands in his moral point of view. It is also a thorough and intellectually informed book. Marine makes good use of such traditional journalistic devices as interviews, ideological digressions, and supporting documents, and he is a talented raconteur. As Senior Editor of *Ramparts* magazine, he is an experienced journalist who is willing to turn his energies to the realization of the new possibilities of journalistic writing, and he brings to his task the sense of what is politically and morally relevant which has come to be associated with his magazine. If *The Black Panthers* seems relatively conventional in form, it is certainly not so with regard to content—it is an unflinching and scrupulously honest document.

Marine's book, like Kozol's and Hersey's, represents an effort on the part of white writers to enlarge upon and correct some of the distorted coverage black Americans have received in established and generally racist newspapers—a problem I discussed in the introduction and elsewhere. Many black voices have been raised during the last few years, and many good new writers are to be numbered among them; but, in general, the voice of significant black journalism has been restricted to shorter pieces published in the underground press. Poets like LeRoi Jones are bringing a new dignity and creativity to black literature; and the political and sociological writing of people like Jones, Malcolm X, Bobby Seale, Stokely Carmichael, Rap Brown, and, particularly, Eldridge Cleaver constitutes an important growth and enrichment of black culture. There are now literally hundreds of readable and helpful books on black Americans, and books like Charles Silberman's *Crisis in Black and White* and William Grier and Price Cobbs' *Black Rage* are especially good. But most of the good *journalism* about black culture has been written by whites, largely out of a concern to discover the truth about racial conflicts that are so easily passed off by the established press as "ghetto riots" or the truth about black political leaders who are pigeonholed simply as "militants." In the final analysis they write in order to fulfill the journalistic ideal of telling what is really happening, to offer the public reliable and useful information for implementing changes in racial relations, and to expiate the sin of their own racism. To write in such a way, as Kozol and Hersey have made clear, requires a radical kind of honesty as well as the modesty to admit one's ignorance and limitations.

Before beginning his account of the Black Panthers, Gene Marine makes some apropos statements:

> "People are not really unconcerned about the problems of blacks," a television news executive told me recently (apparently unaware that blacks *are* people), "and I don't think that they're unwilling to do something about them. It's just that they're tired of hearing about them."
>
> All right. I won't write about the problems of black people. I shall write only about white problems, and in fact only about one of those. That white problem is called the Black Panther Party.
>
> You have seen them, at least on television or in newspaper pictures: black berets, powder-blue turtlenecks, black leather jackets, black pants and shoes (in Los Angeles, white T-shirts bearing the legend "Black Panther Party"), and, where legal, guns. The guns, you have prob-

ably been told, are for police, or for white oppressors, or—perhaps—for you.

Perhaps no white man—and I am white—can adequately convey the background of being black which is necessary in order really to understand the Panthers, who exist now in every major city in America and in quite a few smaller ones. On the other hand, and always excepting a couple of outstanding novelists, if a black man expressed it adequately, he would have to write in black terms, and if you're white, you probably wouldn't understand him anyway.

So I have undertaken to "explain" the Black Panthers, as best I can, as a white reporter writing primarily for other whites. I have no doubt that the alert will find in my account ample evidence of racism—I cannot not be myself, and I am a white American. I can only say that I am aware of the problem, and I've tried. . . . I am a reporter. One with opinions, it is true . . . but a reporter nonetheless. I have done my best in what follows to *report* on the origins and development of the Black Panther Party and on its expressed and implied philosophies, regardless of whether some of the comfortable find the result offensive. To quote a great lady with whom I once worked, Elsa Knight Thompson, "Sometimes the facts are biased."[10]

Marine exemplifies the qualities of honesty and modesty, and, as he says later, he has a good deal of sympathy for the Black Panthers, as well as being frightened by them.

He makes clear from the beginning of the book that the Panthers were originally a force for self-defense against police harassment in the Oakland, California, ghetto. He charges that the Oakland police are bigoted, that the force hires new members on the basis of their bigotry, and that it was harassment and brutality on the part of the police which transformed the Panthers into an increasingly militant organization, not only in Oakland but across the country. They have been also, with their educational and community programs, a force for great good among black Americans in the ghettos, and that good, according to Marine, has been perverted by police activity and by misunderstanding of their organization on the part of most white Americans. That misunderstanding, as he repeats several times, is largely due to the conscious and unconscious racism of the conventional press and media, and he offers the book as a remedial journalistic education. As an intelligent reporter, he knows the facts may be biased, but, as a New Journalist, he knows that a well-articulated and open presentation of facts can make possible the revelation of truth.[11]

Seymour M. Hersh's *My Lai 4: A Report on the Massacre and Its Aftermath* is probably the most revelatory and controversial book yet published on the war in Vietnam. The book concerns the massacre of several hundred civilians at the hamlet of My Lai on March 16, 1968, by the men of Charlie Company—an event now familiar to any American television-viewer. Hersh's work is occasionally inaccurate in small details —a fact which he admits—but no one yet knows exactly what an "accurate" account of the incident will be, though Hersh's must be close. He has been accused of prejudicing the trials which are still not completed, and he may have done that. He, like Hersey, took that chance in order to bring before the American public information to which it is entitled, and the evidence is generally so clear and overwhelming that there is no doubt that the incident occurred approximately as he describes it. He, like many New Journalists, believes that the general truth of an event can be assessed without all the facts having been scientifically and legally processed. Hersh has been criticized because his report is based only on interviews with over fifty men of Charlie Company and because he has never been to Vietnam. Since the Army kept the event secret for over a year and since, after that time, the men involved were all stateside, it seems clear that there would have been little point in his going to My Lai 4; and the delay in responding to the event can hardly be construed as having been Hersh's fault. Given the fact that the Army hid the event so well, and that the bodies of the victims were long buried, there was little left for him to work with but the testimony of several dozen witnesses and accomplices—and he used well the information he obtained.

Hersh, who is a former Chicago police reporter and press secretary to Senator Eugene McCarthy during the 1968 campaign, as well as a Pulitzer Prize-winning journalist, was doing research for a book on the Pentagon when he received a telephone tip about the massacre on October 22, 1969. At that time the Army was trying secretly to court-martial Lt. William Calley, one of the platoon leaders, for killing seventy-five Vietnamese civilians. Hersh went to interview Calley's lawyer and was the first reporter to interview Calley. He then began piecing together and expanding the story of the massacre through other interviews. In his preface Hersh describes the problems of his technique:

> These interviews inevitably produced a maze of conflicting stories: many of the men were unable to agree on details, especially when asked to discuss an event that took place nearly two years earlier and one in which they may have committed premeditated murder.
>
> I tried to balance that advantage three ways.
>
> First, I interviewed as many members of the company as possible to find those facts and incidents that were generally agreed upon. Many Charlie Company members were personally interviewed two or more times, and most were contacted again by telephone to clarify conflicting points.
>
> Second, I was provided with access to a limited number of transcripts of interrogations of key witnesses that were conducted by the Criminal Investigating Division (CID) and the office of the Inspector General, the two Army agencies which did the bulk of the investigation of My Lai 4.
>
> Third, simply trying to ensure that my interviews were accurately reported was not enough, and I decided to censor some statements because either they were obviously contradictory or could not be verified by other witnesses. Where there was a conflict on significant points, that conflict is described as fully as possible.[12]

Hersh's honesty is of the utmost importance to his report, as is his willingness to be open about problems of consistency. He has, I think, used the interview material as effectively as possible in filling in the background information about My Lai 4 and Charlie Company, in portraying the aftermath of the event, and, most critically, in trying to recreate the event itself. Like Capote and Hersey, or like any good journalist, Hersh understands the potentialities and limitations of interview material, and he makes good use of letters written by members of the company as valuable documents about its morale and psychological state. The letters and interviews are supple-

mented with a careful history of Quang Ngai Province, anecdotes about such figures as George S. Patton III, as well as
official communiques, governmental letters, and a plethora of
data about the background of the people involved in the event
and its aftermath.

Hersh carefully demonstrates that it was lack of combat
rather than too much that accounts for Charlie Company's
action at My Lai 4, and he dramatizes the profundity of their
frustrations through statements from individual men, like
Ronald Grzesik:

> "It just started building. I don't know why. Everybody
> reached the point where they were frustrated. We weren't
> getting any action, yet the only thing on our mind was
> survival. After Bill [William Weber] got killed, I began
> to stop caring. I remember writing a letter home saying
> that I once had sympathy for these people, but now I
> didn't care. I became passive: I couldn't beat them up
> but I wouldn't try to stop it. Yet I told Calley at one point
> that I wouldn't question anybody unless he stopped beat-
> ing them up. There'd be days when I'd just be sick of it."
> (37)

As Hersh makes clear, there were conflicting opinions
about what orders the company's captain, Ernest L. Medina,
had given in regard to the treatment of the people in My Lai 4,
but there is little disagreement about what basically happened
there—for whatever reason:

> The killings began without warning. Harry Stanley
> told the CID that one young member of Calley's platoon
> took a civilian into custody and then "pushed the man up
> to where we were standing and then stabbed the man in
> the back with his bayonet. . . . The man fell to the ground
> and was gasping for breath." The GI then "killed him with
> another bayonet thrust or by shooting him with a rifle. . . .
> There were so many people killed that day it is hard for
> me to recall exactly how some of the people died." The
> youth next "turned to where some soldiers were holding
> another forty- or fifty-year-old man in custody." He
> "picked this man up and threw him down a well. Then
> [he] pulled the pin from a M26 grenade and threw it in
> after the man." Moments later Stanley saw "some old

women and some little children—fifteen or twenty of them —in a group around a temple where some incense was burning. They were kneeling and crying and praying and various soldiers . . . walked by and executed these women and children by shooting them in the head with their rifles." (49-50)

The soldiers knew they were not killing VC, and Hersh's account suggests that Medina probably knew there weren't any VC in the village. Hersh brings home the meaning of the massacre more effectively than any of the television news coverage or the pictures in *Life*.

After his original interview with Calley, Hersh tried to sell the interview to various major magazines, all of which expressed little interest, and he finally had to sell it to thirty-five newspapers through the small Dispatch News Service of Washington, D.C. The slowness of the press in responding to the My Lai 4 incident, for which Hersh supplies extensive evidence, was appalling to him and accounted no doubt, in part at least, for his commitment to writing and publishing his report. Like many New Journalists, he discerned the obvious significance of an event which the established press, wittingly or unwittingly, was helping the Army keep undercover, and devoted himself to its transformation into moving and informative journalism.[13]

5

OTHER NEW JOURNALISTS: THE YOUTH AND RADICAL SCENE AND THE NEW MUCKRAKERS

> **Every reporter is a dramatist, creating a theatre out of life.**
>
> Jerry Rubin in
> *Do It!*

The journalism of "the youth and radical scene" is more prolific than that I have discussed under any other heading. I use the word *youth* to imply journalistic writing by and about young people, many students or underground-press writers or both, who may or may not be "radical" in the various senses of that word. Most of these journalists are writing about, or from the perspectives of, the various subcultures of America, most of which are included in Theodore Roszak's counterculture which is seeking alternative styles of life and consciousness, styles which differ, usually "radically," from the conventional, accepted American pattern of religious, social-political, and sexual behavior. Also, some of the best journalists of youth and radical activities are neither young nor radical, nor associated with the underground press, but are simply intelligent and sympathetic writers who realize the significance of those activities.

Having discussed the New Journalism of black nationalism (which technically fits under the present heading) in the previous chapter and in the second chapter, I would like to consider that of the student revolution, rock culture, hippie culture, drug culture, yippie and New Left politics, and communal-rural alternative cultures. Because there is a great deal of New Journalistic writing involved here, I have chosen several representative works to discuss briefly, though in some detail, and have included many others by way of the notes. Again, as in the previous chapter, this is not a comprehensive discussion but is one that I hope takes account of most of the talented and significant New Journalists included under this heading. I also include a short discussion of some other aspects of the New Muckrakers' writing, in an attempt to suggest further its reach and importance.

THE YOUTH AND RADICAL SCENE

Those collective activities which I term "the student revolution" began, for this generation in America, with a complex set of interrelated events. Those events include the Beatles, Bob Dylan, Johnson's escalation of the Vietnam war, drugs—all the exhibits that are usually brought in to support the case. All those exhibits might be lumped together as having contributed to a change in the awareness of young people, and of some older ones as well, of the roles they play in everyday life and of the ways in which those roles could or should be changed or dropped. Most of the people involved in that change of awareness were students, primarily college students, and their first attempt to test the validity of that change publicly and politically, as students, was the Free Speech Movement, which began at the University of California at Berkeley in the fall of 1964. That movement was not simply about "free speech" but about the power of the university and the government over student activities. It was a challenge to the traditional sources of academic and political authority, a challenge that was inevitable with the change of awareness; and Mario Savio and the other students involved demonstrated the kind of power which students might exercise in making their needs heard, in implementing the fulfillment of those needs, and in freeing themselves from the rigidity and insensitivity of authority that was and still is to a great extent irrelevant or oppressive to their development and education as individuals. The activities, on campuses and otherwise, that stem from that event are now a matter of on-going history.

The book which records the Berkeley Free Speech Movement, the granddaddy of virtually all student revolution books, is Hal Draper's *Berkeley: The New Student Revolt* (New York: Grove Press, Inc., 1965). Draper's journalistic account, supported by documents and speeches, is an important historical record, and its success and relevance encouraged the writing of more books about new student political activities, until today there are at least a dozen good books about student politics and a few dozen more lesser ones.[1] Another seminal document is "The Student as Nigger," an article which appeared early in 1967 in the Los Angeles *Free Press*, by Jerry Farber, who was then a teacher at L. A. State College. That article, which he has recently collected with some of his other work in a book, *The Student as Nigger* (North Hollywood, Calif.: Contact Books, 1969), defined and attacked the conventional student-university interface more directly and insightfully than any work prior to its time. Farber's article, which found immediate resonance in its sympathetic readers and incredible dissonance in its opponents, contends that the role of the student vis-à-vis teachers, administrators, and the educational system is clearly analogous to that of the "nigger" in a racist society—he is castrated, manipulated, exploited, feared, hated, and ignored by a similar authoritarian mind-set.

Educated by the events of Berkeley and other schools, by articles and books like Farber's, by a growing awareness of the general condition of the world, and by their own sense of alienation and of the need for reformation and change, university students, and gradually high-school students as well, have been motivated to create an unprecedented pressure for the transformation of the political and educational establishments of America. A typical university student of the late 1960's is considerably more radical in most of his views than his counterpart of the late 1950's or early 1960's, and his political involvement, conventional or unconventional, or disinvolvement is much different; it is usually typified by frustration and moral concern and, frequently, by an activism that is becoming increasingly more militant. There are two books by this new kind of student which strike me both as good examples of New Journalistic writing and as relevant, significant documentations of the student revolution and its people: James Simon Kunen's *The Strawberry Statement: Notes of a College Revolutionary* and Dotson Rader's *I Ain't Marchin' Anymore.*

The Strawberry Statement, which was made into a movie, is basically a journal about the events at Columbia University during the spring and summer of 1968 when SDS and its sympathizers were striking against Columbia's real estate practices and its support of the Institute for Defense Analysis, a consortium of twelve universities engaged in research for the Pentagon. It is also a more general sort of revelation of Kunen and his world. The book was contracted with Random House before he ever wrote it; portions appeared in *New York* magazine and the *Atlantic;* and Kunen sold its movie rights, so he isn't totally disaffiliated from the "system" and is an informative, if sometimes flip, critic of it. Kunen is typically offhand and humorous, somewhat self-debunking but also committed and impatient with inessentials, as the style of his introductory material shows:

> My question is a simple one; who am I to write a book? I don't know. I'm just writing it. You're just reading it. Let's not worry about it. . . .
>
> Writing a book is a lot like having a baby; they both involve bringing something into the world that wasn't there before, and they're both a pain in the ass.
>
> This book was written on napkins and cigarette packs and hitchhiking signs. It was spread all over, but so is my mind. I exhibit a marked tendency to forget things. I can remember only three things at a time. . . .
>
> The best, truest way to read this book would be to rip it up and throw the scraps all over the house. Then, later, should you come across a piece, read it, or don't read it, depending on how you feel. Or, better, save it until four o'clock in the morning when you would rather do almost anything else, and read it then. Above all, don't spend too much time reading it because I didn't spend much time writing it.
>
> You will notice that a great deal of this book simply relates little things I've done and thought. It may seem completely irrelevant to Columbia. That's the way it goes.[2]

Kunen is not a professional writer, but his seeming, and sometimes real, casualness works well as a basis for his style, which is freewheeling, direct, and paced flexibly with the events he describes. He is an imperfect but effective journalist.

The book takes its life from his markedly personal, creative sense of reality—so much so that his occasional objective passages seem very flat by comparison. As several reviewers have noticed, there is something of Huck Finn and Holden Caulfield about Kunen as a narrator—the same innocence and humor, but the same seriousness as well. His collection of vignettes, on-the-scene reportage, musings, anecdotes, and gnomic aphorisms show him, like the conscientious members of SDS, to be a confused but honest and morally concerned person who is searching for and demanding a new humanity from the system in which he lives. He is a sane and perspective reporter, and, in the commentarial portions of the book, he exercises an articulate critical intelligence—an impression one gains also from his recent television appearances.

A good example of Kunen's style is his journal entry for Tuesday, July 30, which also explains the origin of the book's title:

I passed a store called "Hard-to-Get Records." I wonder if they have easy-to-get records. If they don't that makes them hard to get, in which case they should have them.

I wandered up to Columbia and drifted into a Strike Steering Committee meeting.

Mark Rudd, who is among other things Chairman of the Sanitation Committee, was talking.

"The politics has been shitty. The organization has been shitty. The Strike School up to now has been a marshmallow."

With that I went to the *Spectator* offices to satisfy myself that the Strawberry Statement did, in reality, so to speak, exist.

On March 21, 1967, Ralph Halford, Dean of Graduate Faculties, denied any connection between the University and the Institute for Defense Analysis.

Ten days later, the Columbia *Spectator* revealed that Columbia was affiliated, that several faculty members were engaged in secret research, and that there was a secret research facility in Pupin Hall (a building which already bears the distinction of having been the birthplace of the atom bomb).

The article quoted Norman L. Christeller, vice-president and general manager of IDA: "We consider Columbia to be one of the three or four primary sponsors of the IDA. President Kirk has always been an active member of our boards."

That was the golden spike. That was the red button. That was the celestial firing cap, the interstellar trigger mechanism, the electromagnetic ignition key, the super sky switch which blended all the currents which had for so long been wending their way together. From the germination of the first strawberry to the purchase of Manhattan, the birth of Grayson Kirk's maternal great-grandfather to Mark Rudd's application essay on extracurricular activities, the first billy club turning on the lathe, the racial bifurcation of American society—all the myriad particles of history and evolution streaming down the reality cables of the universe. With this revelation all was finally in readiness, and on April 25, 1967, the Strawberry Statement sprang from the lips of Dean Deane, to absolutely no effect whatever.

"A university is definitely not a democratic institution," Professor Deane began. "When decisions begin to be made democratically around here, I will not be here any longer."

Commenting on the importance of student opinion to the administration, Professor Deane declared, "Whether students vote 'yes' or 'no' on an issue is like telling me they like strawberries."

I like strawberries. (139-140)

Kunen has a keen sense of irony, very dry in his reportage of Christeller's proud announcement of the very evidence SDS needed to justify their action against Columbia. His lyrical and metaphoric description of the significance of that evidence is reminiscent of Wolfe or Mailer, and his concluding statement, "I like strawberries," is a summary illustration of the difference between so-called objective and honestly personal journalism. As in the rest of the book, Kunen brings in all manner of things to expand the reader's sense of participation in the events of his world. He himself was very much involved in them (he was one of the people occupying Kirk's office during the strike), and his book communicates beautifully the sense of his involvement.

Dotson Rader's *I Ain't Marchin' Anymore* (which takes its title from a Phil Ochs song) is, like Kunen's book, autobiographical in pose. Like Kunen, Rader is writing about the Columbia strike and the riots and police brutality which followed. He is also writing about the "mobilization for peace" in New York City, the Pentagon march, his own life, and the lives of people around him. His book betrays a disillusionment with protest politics, as the title suggests; he is a much more serious, cynical and, sometimes, pretentious writer than Kunen, though both show an exuberant youthfulness about the sexual games that can be played during political revolutions. He traces his development from a social worker to a political radical who is militantly at war with the American governmental system—an evolution which one can detect also in the shift in the underground press's rhetoric and concerns, as was seen earlier, and which characterizes more and more the political careers of activists in the counterculture. The book is a record of the movement of leftist politics from peaceful and relatively passive protest to a militant and open rebellion whereby the rebel defines himself and his freedom, à la Camus or Franz Fanon, through acts of rebellion and, ultimately, violence.

For Rader, as for his friends and most politically radical students, as well as the Black Panthers, this movement toward militance was and is still being prompted by the militance and numb brutality being forced upon them by the powers that be. It is a self-defensive reaction, no matter what political rhetoric might call it. Rader, in spite of the frequent staleness of his voice, shows himself a good journalist in reporting the kinds of events which served to radicalize him into a militant attitude. He is capable of writing in a style that is immediate to the situation, staccato, personally involved, and moving enough to radicalize, temporarily at least, virtually any reader. Consider, as an example, his account of an incident during the peace demonstrations of 15 April 1967, in New York City:

> We stood at the intersection of 42nd Street and Second Avenue. I was tired. Philip seemed about worn through. The sky was clouding over heavily. Soon it would rain. . . .
>
> A young man in his late teens walked into the intersection against the light. He cried, "Peace Now!" Philip and I waved at him. I thought, he must have just arrived, he must not have seen the bust or he would not shout like that. He must not know what the police have done. He was wearing a light blue shirt and blue pants. His hair was sandy colored. He was about 5'10". As he entered the street he shouted the slogan. That was all he did. Then four pro-war men jumped him. One kicked him in the groin. The young man slumped down as he was kicked.

I thought, you poor bastard, you better just lie there, you better not move. There were many police in the area. The pro-war men ran away. The young man got up and tried to chase after them. You dumb kid, I thought, they'll get you now. We did nothing. As he started up, four policemen suddenly attacked him. They beat him. The young man fell to the street. Philip said, "Good Christ, they're animals." The young man got up. They hit him again. He broke free of the police and ran uptown along Second Avenue toward 43rd Street, weaving dazed to the right and left. We followed him as he ran. About a third of the way to 43rd the police caught him. We saw the police beat him senseless, using their fists, not their clubs, feeling the thud of the knuckle against the stomach. Nice. Finally they knocked him unconscious, dropping him bloody against the curb. They looked about, daring any spectators to intervene. We were within ten feet of the young man. We jeered at the police, my head throbbing as I yelled, saying, "Shame!" and "Bullies!" We wanted them to leave the young man alone. And then, unable ever to release a victim, they lifted the unconscious boy. Two officers dragged him to a mounted policeman nearby. They lifted the limp body nearly as high as the saddle of the horse. The young man's bleeding head was slumped forward, his chin resting on his chest. I could see the blood slipping out under his shirt sleeve and running down his hand and dripping on to the pavement. While the two patrolmen held him the mounted trooper raised his nightstick above his head and brought it down on the boy's skull swiftly. He hit him very hard. We heard the crack of the wooden club against his skull. A woman screamed. Philip said, "My God, it's incredible!" My stomach began to hurt. We were frightened. They dropped the body to the pavement. He was bleeding heavily. The police pushed us away. For the first time in his life Philip was terrified of the cops. Their violence unprovoked. Obscene. Cheap.[3]

What Rader observes and reports is frightening, and he captures it well. The passage is visually and viscerally real, the future it suggests, apocalyptic.

Another part of the youth scene is rock culture—rock

music, its musicians, its audience, and the cultural environment it creates. The term "rock journalism" refers to the journalism which is about rock culture, and it is, I think, an important part of the New Journalism. Because rock music has become a much more creative and far-reaching cultural force than it was in the 1950's, there has naturally come about a journalism which is partly music criticism and sociology, partly popular philosophy and cultural history, that attempts to cover and interpret the rock scene.

Contemporary rock, like so many other revolutionary forces now active in America, emerged as part of the complex change in awareness that began in the mid-1960's with student protest, radical politics, drugs, sexual freedom, and the rest of that intricate historical gestalt. The single most obvious cause, at first anyway, was undoubtedly LSD, although the more prototypical one is the need for a new music which always accompanies radical cultural change—no matter how one might analyze that need into its component manifestations. The decline of acid rock in the late 1960's denies that LSD has been a continuous motive force in rock music, though the art forms, mysticisms, and experimental life-styles of drug culture have had a great influence on the music, just as much of the music has itself promoted drug culture. It is important to remember, however, that rock is a complex force, a mode of communal consciousness and participation that is integrated with various forms of freedom and vision. Thus, rock journalism is a very eclectic journalism, one which demands of its writers both a thorough intellectual grasp of rock's significance, as music and as a cultural force, and a sensuous awareness of its subtleties, changes, and emotional and spiritual power as a personal experience.

Ralph J. Gleason, a good rock journalist and an associate editor of *Rolling Stone,* probably the best rock newspaper in the United States (see my discussion in chapter two), relates the development of rock journalism to the growth of FM underground radio in the San Francisco area, the center of rock activity in the mid-1960's:

A whole new radio concept emerged from this. KMPX played tapes, it played cuts from albums regardless of length and it played music that was never listed on the Top-40 stations. It ran announcements of lost dogs, astrological forecasts and plugs for dances which were benefits for everything from the Free Medical Clinic to artists whose studios had been burned out or appeals for student demonstration bail funds.

"Underground radio" was the name and it spawned imitations all over the country—there are now [1969] upward of 70 such stations programing, to a greater or lesser degree, this kind of music. The advertisements that support the underground press are all basically a result of what this radio concept showed—that there is a mass adult audience for nonteenybopper (or bubble-gum) music which is also pop rock. . . .

As FM radio emerged in the new form in San Francisco, so did rock journalism. Back as far as the early fifties, the *Chronical* [sic] had encouraged me to interview and write about current pop performers. When Elvis Presley did one of his only concerts back in 1956 at the Oakland Auditorium, I interviewed him and reviewed the show. Fats Domino, Hank Williams, Bill Doggett, Paul Anka, Buddy Holly, Ray Charles all were covered by the *Chronicle.* Then with the upsurge of pop-folk, Peter, Paul & Mary and the Kingston Trio and the music they represented was added. The *Chronicle* coverage of Bob Dylan was the most extensive press coverage and criticism he had received up to that time.

So it was natural to follow logically into rock with reviews of the big Cow Palace shows and the people appearing there and at subsequent events.

But at the end of 1967, as FM emerged, so did a magazine-newspaper called *Rolling Stone,* edited by Jann Wenner, a University of California student who had conducted a rock column almost from the beginning of the rock renaissance in *The Daily Californian.* Later, when I was on the *Ramparts* editorial board and *Sunday Ramparts,* which existed as a weekly hip newspaper for a year or so, was being formed, Wenner came to it as entertainment editor.

Rolling Stone was Wenner's idea. In the fall of 1967, with Michael Lydon, now a New York *Times* writer, and myself it was launched and has since become the most influential voice in the rock field. . . .[4]

The primary function of underground radio was to make the new music available for the continuous listening of a new audience and for its critics, so that it became more public and accessible as an art form and way of life to be written about.

With the rise of Bob Dylan, the Beatles, the Rolling Stones, and San Francisco groups like the Jefferson Airplane and the Grateful Dead, more concerts were given and, as Gleason says, the FM underground spread; rock journalism grew into its own. Almost all popular and underground newspapers and magazines with any appreciable circulation now carry rock journalism of some kind, whether it be only occasional reviews of new records or lengthy accounts of rock activities; and many new rock periodicals are now being published, from underground-type papers to mod, glossy magazines.

Having discussed *Rolling Stone* and *Crawdaddy* in chapter two, and having here sketched in the background of rock journalism, I would like to mention briefly some of its representative and most talented writers and their work.

There are several good book-length works, of which Gleason's *The Jefferson Airplane and the San Francisco Sound,* quoted above, is a good example. Gleason is very sympathetic with rock culture, and his enthusiasm infects the reader with the culture's energy and meaning. Hunter Davies' *The Beatles* (New York: McGraw-Hill Book Co., 1968) is a thorough biography of the group, as well as an intimate New Journalistic account of their recent creative and personal lives, well documented through Davies' living out his Boswellian role close to the Beatles for over a year. It is a key book, both because of the style of its journalism and because of its record of the cultural milieu of the single most important group in the history of contemporary rock. An earlier rock *Geistesgeschichte,* or ideological history, is Arnold Shaw's *The Rock Revolution* (New York: Macmillan Co., 1967), and a more recent one is Jerry Hopkins' *The Rock Story* (New York: New American Library, 1970). Both are very readable accounts, partly retrospective and partly immediate and personal, of the evolution of rock music and its cultural context.

There are two particularly good anthologies of article-length writing about rock culture which include some good journalistic work as well as more philosophical discussions. *The Age of Rock: Sounds of the American Cultural Revolution,* edited by *Commonweal* editor Jonathan Eisen (New York: Random House, Inc., 1969), is a fountain of some of the best pieces from *Crawdaddy, Cheetah, Ramparts,* and the *Village Voice,* as well as such journals as *The American Scholar;* and it includes many of the best rock journalists of the 1960's, such as Nat Hentoff, Ralph J. Gleason, Richard Poirer, and Jon Landau. *Rock and Roll Will Stand,* edited by *Rolling Stone* writer Greil Marcus (Boston: Beacon Press, 1969), is also a good collection. It contains some intelligent history-of-ideas writing as well as some rock journalism from the underground press.[5]

The most important aspect of the youth and radical scene is its character as a counterculture, borrowing Theodore Roszak's term again. As a counterculture, it stands in clear opposition or indifference to the major American cultural and political scene. The student revolution and rock culture are certainly part of this counterculture, but there are other subcultures which, while they overlap these two, may also be distinguished from them in important ways. Hippie subculture, which is primarily an urban phenomenon, differs from both in its disaffiliation from the university and from at least the glossier aspects of rock culture, although, as I admit, this is a hazy distinction qualified by exceptions. An analogous remove from the student revolution and from rock culture can be discerned in the subcultures of people, primarily young, who are devoted to turn-on's like Zen and yoga, to experimenting with life-styles that involve dropping out of the system to the extent of returning to primitive and rural communes, to ultra-radical and full-time revolutionary politics, or to the pursuit of an anarchic and openly criminal life-style. All of these subcultures represent countercultural possibilities, alternatives to conventional and generally accepted ways of living, thinking, and feeling, in which many activist students and rock-culture people may or may not participate.

With the realization of these cultural alternatives there has come about a journalism which has been developing alongside and concerning itself with them and their people. Some of this journalism has been written by those involved in realizing these alternatives, some by sympathetic outsiders. Most of it is to be found in the publications of the underground press, but the best of it has appeared elsewhere.

Hunter Thompson's *Hell's Angels: A Strange and Terrible Saga* is a classic example of New Journalistic writing about the people of a particular subculture. Thompson's book has the thoroughness and documentation of Gene Marine's *The Black Panthers,* but Thompson is personally and stylistically closer to the experiences he reports and is frequently as scintillating and creative a stylist as Tom Wolfe. Thompson was a free-lance novelist and a journalist who had written for several magazines and the New York *Herald Tribune* when he first became involved with the Hell's Angels in 1964. Out of that encounter he wrote an article on them, "Motorcycle Gangs: Losers and Outsiders" (*Nation,* 17 May 1965, pp. 522-26), which was probably the first piece of honest writing about the Angels done by any known journalist for a major publication. He stayed close to their activities, riding and living with them, for several more months—a total of about a year's time into 1966—until they finally beat him up because they considered him to be using them; then he completed the book.

Thompson's book is an especially significant document of the New Journalism, because it came about in large part because of his desire to correct the reportage of the established media, to get close to a way of life and write about it as it really is. The distorted portrait of Hell's Angels which the average American held before him in his living-room chair was, according to Thompson, a creation of the established press of New York City—a portrait which the Angels disastrously tried to live up to:

> The Hell's Angels as they exist today were virtually created by *Time, Newsweek* and *The New York Times.* The *Times* is the heavyweight champion of American journalism. On nine stories out of ten the paper lives up to its reputation. Yet the editors make no claim to infallibility, and now and then they will blow the whole duke. It would be senseless to try to list these failures, and besides that the purpose of this harangue is not to nail any one newspaper or magazine—but to point out the potentially massive effect of any story whose basic structure is endorsed and disseminated not only by *Time* and *Newsweek,* but by the hyper-prestigious *New York Times.* The *Times* took the Lynch report [the pseudo-objective and vague report of an investigation mounted by California's ambitious new

Attorney General Thomas C. Lynch, concerning Hell's Angels and "other disreputables"] at face value and simply reprinted it in very condensed form. The headline said: CALIFORNIA TAKES STEPS TO CURB TERRORISM OF RUFFIAN CYCLISTS. The bulk of the article was straight enough, but the lead was pure fiction: "A hinterland tavern is invaded by a group of motorcycle hoodlums. They seize a female patron and rape her. Departing, they brandish weapons and threaten bystanders with dire reprisals if they tell what they saw. Authorities have trouble finding a communicative witness, let alone arresting and prosecuting the offenders."

This incident never occurred. It was created, as a sort of journalistic montage, by the correspondent who distilled the report. But the *Times* is neither written nor edited by fools, and anyone who has worked on a newspaper for more than two months knows how technical safeguards can be built into even the wildest story, without fear of losing reader impact. What they amount to, basically, is the art of printing a story without taking legal responsibility for it. The word "alleged" is a key to this art. Other keys are "so-and-so said" (or "claimed"), "it was reported" and "according to." In fourteen short newspaper paragraphs, the *Times* story contained nine of these qualifiers. The two most crucial had to do with the Hollywood lead and the " '*alleged* gang rape' last Labor Day of two girls, 14 and 15 years old, by five to ten members of the Hell's Angels gang on the beach at Monterey" (my italics). . . . The result was a piece of slothful, emotionally biased journalism, a bad hack job that wouldn't have raised an eyebrow or stirred a ripple had it appeared in most American newspapers . . . but the *Times* is a heavyweight even when it's wrong, and the effect of this article was to put the seal of respectability on a story that was, in fact, a hysterical, politically motivated accident.[6]

Thus, Thompson set out to find the true story of the Angels, propelled by a desire to find out what was really happening in their world, to experience it as much as possible as they did, and then to write the story in a style true to his sense of the experience.

Thompson uses police reports and fallacious or true news reports as effective documents in his account, and he has a genuine talent for using epigraphic material; but, besides those facts and his thoroughness, it is his style that distinguishes the book as reportage and makes it a New Journalistic work of art that reminds one of Wolfe and is probably influenced by him. Consider, for example, the opening lines:

> California, Labor Day weekend . . . early, with ocean fog still in the streets, outlaw motorcyclists wearing chains, shades and greasy Levis roll out from damp garages, all-night diners and cast-off one-night pads in Frisco, Hollywood, Berdoo and East Oakland, heading for the Monterey peninsula, north of Big Sur . . . The Menace is loose again, the Hell's Angels, the hundred-carat headline, running fast and loud on the early morning freeway, low in the saddle, nobody smiles, jamming crazy through traffic and ninety miles an hour down the center stripe, missing by inches . . . like Genghis Khan on an iron horse, a monster steed with a fiery anus, flat out through the eye of a beer can and up your daughter's leg with no quarter asked and none given; show the squares some class, give em a whiff of those kicks they'll never know. . . . (11)

The style is perfectly attuned to the subject matter, and Thompson keeps it true, modulating and adapting it throughout to different situations and different aspects of his reportage. Finally, at the end, after he has been beaten to the extent of spitting blood and is kept awake by the pain of a broken rib, he cannot think of a fitting original epitaph for the story and so recalls Conrad: "The horror! The horror! . . . Exterminate all the brutes!" His sympathies have come full circle, his experience to completion. His story is about a kind of rough splendor. It is also about meanness and brutality. But he has, at any rate, written of the Angels as they really are and has done them journalistic justice.

Like Hell's Angels, student activism, and many of the best American rock groups, hippie culture was born and came of age in California, especially in the San Francsico-Berkeley area. It was also proclaimed in a public "funeral" in 1967 that it died there; and it is certainly true that much of its gentleness, innocence, and beauty did die in that year, although the historical changes it began are still in process. Hippie subculture was and, to the extent that it still exists, is associated with other subcultures, particularly those involving various kinds of turned-on life-styles, whether that turning-on comes about through drugs like LSD, mescaline, marijuana, and speed, used either for kicks or as a religious sacrament, or through mysticism, Zen, Krishna consciousness, or any of a dozen other modes of sensory and spiritual awareness. There are many books dealing with these phenomena of hippie and turned-on life-styles, but very few that are good journalism. I would like to discuss four I think are worthwhile: Nicholas von Hoffman's *We Are the People Our Parents Warned Us Against*, William J. Craddock's *Be Not Content*, Jane Kramer's *Allen Ginsberg in America*, and Rasa Gustaitis' *Turning On*.

In 1967, when he completed *We Are the People Our Parents Warned Us Against*, Nicholas von Hoffman was a reporter for the Washington *Post*, a former reporter for the Chicago *Daily News*, and a former associate director of Saul Alinsky's Industrial Areas Foundation. He had previously written widely on topical issues, with an examination of Southern racism, *Mississippi Notebook* (1964), to his credit. He was well prepared professionally to write a book about San Francisco's Haight-Ashbury hippie culture. He spent a great deal of time in the area, especially during the 1967 "summer of love," and during that time he saw and recorded the whole range of events that marked both the fruition and the beginning of the decline of hippie culture. While always distanced somewhat from the experiences he reports—perhaps partly because of his own age and life-style or partly because of the cynicism which one detects arising in him once he has seen the brutality, exploitation, failure, and shattered lives, as well as the beauty, that were the Haight-Ashbury scene—he has nonetheless written a remarkably thorough and moving piece of journalism.[7]

Von Hoffman writes of Haight-Ashbury as having both an exotic kind of beauty and a sordid, ghetto-like ugliness. He sees all of the ambiguities of his subject, much as Gene Marine and Hunter Thompson did, though in general his book, in narrative style, is somewhere in between theirs, perhaps closer to Marine's. He portrays the lives and catches the voices of dozens of different people, placing them together in a story that brings the hippie culture to life. He tends not to betray his personal presence, unlike Thompson and more like Marine, and he is very talented as a recreator of scenes. His style is frequently rather conventionally prosaic, though he captures the argot of the people well and occasionally writes prose that is very close to the event it describes or sometimes poetic, as in the opening pages where, as in the rest of the book, he makes effective use of news releases to counterpoint his own writing:

> 1,000 TEST LIFE STRAIN IN SHELTER
> Athens, Ga., Aug. 27 (UPI)—One thousand volunteers, ranging in age from six months to eighty years old, entered a makeshift underground fallout shelter yesterday to see if they can withstand the strain of living together for 24 hours.
> The fog came every day and destroyed the sunshine, and then the Haight was left to itself. News from the outside world sparked discontinuous. It flashed through the airy water like a stoned head flashes on a mandala, or on the nervous face of a straight. The fog and drugs filter out precision, leave a mood, an apocalyptic premonition.[8]

He then picks up this vignette two paragraphs later and begins to release some of its moral implications:

> There were reports of bats dying of unknown causes in the Carlsbad Caverns of New Mexico and of people dying of known causes in Vietnam, Nigeria, Detroit, and Bolivia. These were the reverberations from the other side of the fog, the mountains and the sea, wicked emanations from the world of Maya, from the oneiric life of American illusion. The prophets, the seers, and the magicians of the Haight knew that on their side of the mountain, where the fog blinded people from distraction, it was the center of the good vibrations, the creative energies, the self-effacing self, the cosmogonic infinity. (10)

So, from the beginning he observes a morally ironic quality about the scene, a quality which is apotheosized in the fact that Haight-Ashbury lives in a continuous state of paranoia about drugs, and yet the very illegality of those drugs is what brings money into the community. The paranoia and the pushers and the dealers of drug traffic, the runaway teenagers, the exploitation of tourists by the culture, and the exploitation of the culture by tourists—the whole complex of factors which kept Haight-Ashbury economically alive also was cancerous enough to contribute to its downfall when the drug market fell through, the police came for the runaways, and the tourists left at the end of the summer. Von Hoffman discerns the paradoxes of beauty and ugliness lucidly and communicates an honest story of their interactions.

William J. Craddock's *Be Not Content* is described on the cover as "A Subterranean Journal" and is, like Von Hoffman's book, with which it makes an interesting comparison, concerned with the hippie and drug subcultures of the San Francisco area. Craddock was much more intimately involved with the people and events of which he writes than was Von Hoffman. In a short preface Craddock describes his book as "Excerpts from the Life of Abel Egregore":

> Being a skeletal history and chronicle of the experiences of a single, minor freak connected to a single, minor tribe of acid freaks in California, beginning in the early days of the Psychedelic Revolution, including a brief sampling of an insignificant number of individuals involved, their ideas and their ideals, and a flickering glimpse of but a scant few of the problems, obstacles, superstitions, fears, mis-understandings, joys, insights, loves and frustrations that they faced, manufactured and struggled with in their once pure quest for the elusive path to even more elusive en-lightenment in a set constructed exclusively of intricate but obvious illusions of which they occasionally (with in-finite sadness, regretting the revelation) realized that they were undeniably a micro-part.[9]

Abel Egregore, with whose journal the reader is concerned, is, we assume, a mask worn by Craddock to narrate experiences that are essentially autobiographical.

The book opens in chapter thirty-two with Abel, who has been writing his journal, awakening. Shortly thereafter his friend Curt, while stoned, begins reading Abel's manuscript, and chapter one begins. The journal, theoretically not altered by Curt's state of mind, is a long account of Abel's experiences from high school to the end of the "summer of love" in Septem-ber 1967. He narrates the story of his leaving Hell's Angels for the gentle life-style of the hippies. He meets a mystical girl named Julia, with whom he goes through a poignant and mysterious love experience. He becomes involved with drugs and takes LSD almost continuously, and he makes the nude-bathing and natural-joy scenes at Big Sur and the demonstrations at Berkeley, all the time staying close to the experiences in his writing, recreating everyone's dialog and moods, reporting endlessly all manner of observations, conversations, and encounters. Then in San Francisco he lives through the summer of 1967, the trips festivals, recording elaborately the quest he and his friends are undertaking as well as his own misapprehensions and happinesses. As his use of drugs becomes more obsessive, the style shifts toward a surrealistic, hallucinatory language and pace which reflects his desperation and deep but confused experiences. Finally the journal breaks off in a stupor of fatigue and hope on 7 September 1967. Chapter thirty-two then picks up again, with Curt reading the manuscript.

What the manuscript-journal—of which another friend, Eddie, ate all but one chapter, which he hid—attempts to narrate is one person's experience of the hippie-drug culture—an attempt which is essentially New Journalistic in achievement, whether or not Craddock intended it to be journalism. He, like Von Hoffman, shows some feelings of skepticism about the hippie-drug culture. He is also aware of the ambiguities at play in such cultural experiments, but his account differs from Von Hoffman's in its immediacy and sense of involvement; and if his sight isn't quite as journalistically clear as Von Hoffman's, his affirmations are certainly more intense.

Allen Ginsberg in America, the title patterned after John Malcolm Brinnin's *Dylan Thomas in America,* is written by Jane Kramer, a former staff reporter for the *Village Voice.*[10] The book grew out of an article she had done on Ginsberg entitled "Profiles: A. Ginsberg" (*New Yorker,* 17 August 1968, pp. 32 ff; and 24 August 1968, pp. 38 ff). Although it consists primarily of recent biographical material, it is also about Ginsberg's milieu. Kramer spent a great deal of time with Ginsberg, attending gatherings with him, watching and listening to him day after day, talking to him about his life, so that her story has a very contemporary context, more than a past-historical one—although there is a good deal of background information— and is basically a New Journalistic work in which she is indirectly present as a sympathetic interpretive narrator. She is not an experimental stylist in the way that Wolfe or Hunter Thompson is, but she is a good writer of clean and economical prose. She is very explanatory, so that the book is available to a wide audience—an important fact, given the need to clarify for the non-hip reader the complex controversies and exotic activities associated with Ginsberg. She communicates beautifully the whole man, whether he is chanting mantras or hungry for hamburgers, and she records carefully the environment in which Ginsberg moves, whether it is a be-in in San Francisco or a vacation with his parents at home in Paterson, New Jersey.

Ginsberg's conversations are of central importance to the book's success and meaning as journalism, and Kramer is an adept recorder of his speech and its context. Consider, as an example, her recreation of an encounter between Ginsberg and Andy Warhol. Warhol seldom says anything in public, and Kramer effectively captures the flatness of the moment, Ginsberg's gentle inability to cope with the situation:

> "*Hare Krishna,*" Ginsberg said, giving Warhol a slap on the back.
>
> Warhol winced slightly, and he continued staring at Miss Morse as she flapped her arms in imitation of a tuna death throe. At the end of her story, Warhol uttered a low, carefully modulated "wow." The word was ambiguous as to its moral stance.
>
> Miss Morse flapped on to another booth.
>
> "Well, that's the fishing business," Ginsberg said.
>
> Warhol nodded, moving his head to the right by about a quarter of an inch. A lock of his hair, which was dyed a dry, silvery white, drooped slowly down onto his forehead, and his eyes, which, like Miss Morse's eyes, were very nearly hidden by a pair of dark sunglasses, blinked once. He was wearing a thin striped T-shirt, dungarees, black motorcycle boots, and a look of relentless passivity. A layer of thick, chalky make-up on Warhol's nose was beginning to melt.
>
> "Well, you're looking the same," Ginsberg said cheerfully.
>
> Warhol nodded again.[11]

Kramer also records him at his best, as when he is talking to a young reporter at Berkeley: " 'Don't you know that power's a hallucination?' he said. 'The civil rights movement, Sheriff Rainey, *Time Magazine,* McNamara, Mao—it's all a hallucination. No one can get away with saying that's real. All public reality's a script, and anybody can write the script the way he wants'" (86).

Kramer portrays the character and paradoxes of Ginsberg with great sensitivity:

> Ginsberg, reading and teaching at colleges, has been one of the very few links between the classroom and the communal pad. He is a funny, eloquent teacher, and an admitted ham. As a reader, he is by rapid turns rapturous, weepy, plaintive, outraged, comical, heartbreaking, and then rapturous again. . . . He likes to complain about the frantic life he leads. He says that sometimes, in the middle of a reading, he longs for the simple, private pleasures of a homey Hindu kirtan or a sacred orgy among friends, and he talks about escaping to the woods to write for a year or two. But this is a move that he has always managed to postpone. His own sadhana is as a public man, and offered an option out, he inevitably ignores it and moves on. (93, 94)

Thus, *Allen Ginsberg in America* is a book about a very self-collected man who is nonetheless "on the move," who is trying to bring a gentle and creative order to a world in violent chaos and sickness. Kramer's narrative is deliberate and informing, a journalism devoted to understanding, concerned with coming to terms with Ginsberg and his world—like the man who continues to live beyond her story.

The books and articles now available dealing with drug culture, mysticism, and other aspects of religious and sensuous awareness are numbered in the hundreds. Most are by "experts" of one kind or another, either insiders or outsiders, professional prophets, acid heads, researchers, swamis, and existential or gestalt psychologists. There are also numerous journalistic accounts of experiences concerned with turned-on life-styles in both the underground and popular presses. I have chosen to discuss Rasa Gustaitis' *Turning On* because it strikes me as a uniquely important work of New Journalism: it is a story by a "straight" reporter who enters the turned-on world with unjaded, if, as she admits, prejudiced vision and is transformed through an educational experience which she communicates through her participatory reportage.

In her foreword Gustaitis discusses her own life and what led her to undertake a book on the turned-on scene:

> In the spring of 1967 it was time for another trip. So I looked for a writing assignment that would take me out of New York and to some scenic spot for a couple of the hot months. Nothing interesting came to mind until I heard of Esalen Institute in California, where experiments were being conducted in consciousness expansion without the use of drugs. Indirectly, I heard about Esalen through Clay Felker, editor of *New York Magazine,* who sent me to do a story on a weekend encounter group run by Dr. William C. Schutz. It was the first time I ever heard of either Schutz or encounter groups. At this time, twelve people were to meet in a Bronx mansion and spend two days together being entirely honest with each other in context of that time and place. I went with an extremely negative attitude. For Schutz was a psychologist and I expected to find a lot of dull, neurotic people talking about anxiety, penis envy and their mothers, wallowing in self-pity for two interminable days.
>
> But the weekend turned out to be a mind-bender. I got so involved with that group of strangers (all normal neurotics like me), I felt so strongly about them by Sunday, that it seemed we had been shut up together not two days but two years. . . .
>
> In recent years, many social reformers lost faith in the possibility of change through the political process and sought them through demonstrations, civil disobedience and the disruption of government machinery. But as the Vietnam war and racial guerilla warfare in the cities continued to grow, even direct action of this sort began to seem futile.
>
> And so people—especially young people—who, under other circumstances, might have become political leaders, now withdrew completely from the political process and began to look for areas where individual effort and dedication would yield creative satisfaction. They turned their energies to themselves and their immediate surroundings. Travelers on the turn-on circuit tend to be

apolitical but interested in social experiments such as communes, tribal and extended families. They talk a lot about building world peace through the search for personal peace. . . .

During the summer and fall of 1967 and into the winter, I visited many of these places and people. I got to know psychologists, mystics, hippies, Zen practitioners and individuals who belonged to no group at all but practiced the new style of life in their own fashion. Everywhere I heard of other names and places that were relevant to the general theme but it was impossible to visit all of them. Almost everywhere I participated rather than just observing.[12]

The book she wrote about these experiences is a remarkable document not only of her own education but of the "places and people" involved in it. She participated in group experiments at Esalen; took an LSD trip; attended a hippie wedding ceremony at Big Sur; lived at the Morningstar Ranch commune; listened to the Maharishi Mahesh Yogi; went through a course in Zen training at a monastery; sat in on a sensitivity-training exercise with Charlotte Selver; and experienced brain-wave control in the laboratory of Joseph Kamiya, among other things. She reports all of it with openness and sensitivity in a rich and adaptable style.

As Gustaitis says in her foreword, as her book illustrates, and as any aware American citizen must know by now, many people, particularly the young, are opting out of the corruptions and rigidities of this country's accepted ways of living. It is, of course, a paradoxical, sometimes morally ambiguous maneuver, because most of them don't leave the country and are fundamentally still dependent on it as a technological and economic system—but that is true only if one is willing to grant the painful realities of nationalism, and many of them aren't. For the most part, though, the experiments with new cultural ideals and life-styles are well intentioned, sometimes beautifully vital and hopeful, sometimes failed and cynical. These experiments increasingly have less and less to do with drugs and more to do with returning to the natural landscape and the integrity of being religiously alive to oneself and the environment. Thus, as Gustaitis notes, one finds communal farms, ranches, and schools everywhere, places where people have gathered to live together in an attempt to find a viable alternative to the sickness of contemporary American life.

Those who opt to work to change the American sociopolitical system have some sympathy for the communal experiments but are basically concerned either with revolutionary, and ultimately violent, political activity or with more moderate and patient reformation efforts. The moderate position is irrelevant to communalists and under attack as passively "liberal" by the advocates of political revolution, violent or otherwise. Since the range of the moderate position is well known to any television viewer or newspaper reader, I would like to discuss briefly some of the New Journalism having to do with the two alternatives of peaceful communal life and revolutionary political activity which offer themselves as the existential extremities of the present and the future.

There are many New Journalistic articles dealing with communal life, although to my knowledge there is only one good book on the subject. One of the best articles from the underground press is Hog Farm leader Hugh Romney's "The Hog Farm," which appeared in the *Realist,* December 1969, and is reprinted in *Countdown,* No. 2 (April 1970), pp. 94-47 (numbered backwards). It is a hip and imaginative personal account of the Kesey-Prankster-like commune's experiences and travels around the country. Two of the best articles in popular magazines are: "Open Land: Getting Back to the Communal Garden," *Harper's,* June 1970, pp. 91-102, an excellent piece about the Wheeler Ranch commune north of San Francisco and the Freedom Farm at an unnamed place in the northwestern United States, by Sara Davidson, who has done some admirable New Journalistic writing for the magazine; and "If Mr. Thoreau Calls, Tell Him I've Left the Country," *Atlantic,* May 1970, pp. 72-85, a fresh and creative report of commune life in Vermont, by Raymond Mungo, ex-director of Liberation News Service. The one book is *The Alternative: Communal Life in New America* (New York: Macmillan Co., 1970), by William Hedgepeth, a senior editor of *Look,* with photographs by Dennis Stock, a photoessayist and film maker from Magnum Photos, Inc. The book is concerned with a number of communal families now surviving in America, and is a well-done work. Hedgepeth's informed text is both reportorial and sociological and is in close touch with its subject; Stock's photography is superb.

The New Journalism of revolutionary politics is everywhere, especially in the underground press, where the best is found. Revolutionary politics are necessarily a part of much New Journalistic writing because they are very much a part of the contemporary political scene, more so since the march on the Pentagon and the riots in Chicago. Besides black radical writers, there are many white journalists of revolutionary politics. Two who are also involved as activist leaders are Abbie Hoffman and Jerry Rubin.

Hoffman's *Revolution for the Hell of It* (New York: Dial Press, Inc., 1968), which he wrote under the pseudonym "Free," is basically a collection of his assorted ravings, but there is some insightful and clever material—as well as some good journalism about such things as the march on the Pentagon. Hoffman's journalistic writing is clearly biased much of the time, but he is trying to detect the center of the events he describes, to make them matter in a way unfamiliar to the established press, and to see in them the vitalities which make them revolutionarily significant. Like many New Journalists, he is a very personal, imaginative writer, and he is usually very honest in his reportage, making his revolutionary bias clear. A newspaper account of an event he covers might contain more factual data, but it won't have the humor, immediacy, and gut-level relevance of his writing. At the very least, his journalism comprises a significant counterpole against which to measure established press reportage.

Similar statements could be made about Hoffman's *Woodstock Nation* (New York: Random House, Inc., 1969) and Jerry Rubin's *Do It!* (New York: Simon and Schuster, 1970). *Woodstock Nation* is Hoffman's answer to Mailer's *Of a Fire on the Moon:* Hoffman considers his book more relevant for his generation because it is about bringing people together on earth rather than shooting them into space. The book was obviously put together very rapidly, but it is a good example of the sort of fast-paced and insightful, if occasionally sloppy, journalism that many underground and revolutionary writers practice. It is also an interesting experiment with mixed typographic styles. Jerry Rubin, who along with Hoffman helped create the yippies, an amalgamation of hippie and New Left life-styles, was a reporter for the Cincinnati *Post and Times-Star* before he became a revolutionary politician; and *Do It!*, for all its nonjournalistic content, shows him to be a good journalist, a better one than Hoffman and probably more conscientious. His coverage of the People's Park incident at Berkeley is among the best I have read, and that of the Chicago riots incisive and frightening.[13]

THE NEW MUCKRAKERS

As we have seen, many of the New Journalists qualify in one degree or another as muckrakers. I have termed New Muckrakers those who respond to the impulse to know and communicate the whole and detailed truth about events, people, or institutions. Most New Journalists fit that category somewhat incidentally, as a consequence of their desire to write honestly and thoroughly. There are some, however, who start with the intention of exposure or revelation as a means of shocking and educating their audience and, hopefully, spurring its members to relevant action; and those journalists I would refer to more formally as New Muckrakers. They are "new" because they represent the renewal and redevelopment of an old tradition in journalism, because there are now a large number of such journalists—enough to constitute a stronger force for this kind of public education than ever before—and because they have various new means for implementing the discovery and verification of their information (which amounts in part to the fact of widespread and obvious corruption, injustice, exploitation, and so forth, in the extant political and technological systems).

The number of books and articles now in print concerning the CIA, military activities and corruptions in Vietnam and stateside, political injustice, racial repression, governmental-industrial back scratching, and problems of that kind is myriad. Such material makes good popular reading, even if it doesn't always spur people to action; but there are certain writers and documents which stand out as especially important to this resurgence of muckraking, and I would like to discuss a few of them briefly.

A trend-setting work is Ralph Nader's *Unsafe at Any Speed* (New York: Grossman Publishers, Inc., 1965), a studied documentation of the failure of the automobile industry to take into account passenger safety in favor of quick production, esthetic appeal, and profits. Paul Ehrlich's *The Population Bomb* (New York: Ballantine Books, Inc., 1968), concerning the inevitability of disaster accompanying the present growth of population, pollution, careless agriculture practice, and nuclear proliferation, is another. Articles and books by such men as Nader and Ehrlich themselves comprise a new and apocalyptically significant journalism, and they have inspired hundreds of journalists, professional and otherwise, to pick up the torch of education and warning. Another important book is *Rebellion and Repression* (New York and Cleveland: World Publishing Co., 1969), Tom Hayden's testimony before the National Commission on the Causes and Prevention of Violence and the House Un-American Activities Committee, which exposes much of the ruthless law-enforcement practice in this country. (Hayden's book was first published in *Hard Times* [formerly *Mayday*] in March 1969. *Hard Times* is the most intelligent and genuinely informative muckraking paper now being published. It is edited by Andrew Kopkind and James Ridgeway, with Fred Gardner and Ralph Nader as consulting editors.) James Ridgeway's *The Closed Corporation* (New York: Random House, Inc., 1968), an exposé of the mutual involvements of universities and the military-industrial complex, is likewise an important book, one which has helped motivate a great deal of student activism. Nader and his "raiders" are now publishing additional books about pollution and urban problems, and the list grows from other quarters as well, with books like Joe McGinnis' *The Selling of the President 1968* (New York: Trident Press, 1969), an examination of the promotional processes that led to the election of the image of Richard Nixon.

What all of this information leads to is at best a new public awareness with an attendant demand for political action and relevant change, as well as a transformation of the dangerous habits of needless luxury and ignorance by which most Americans live. At worst, it will contribute to the information glut and the narcotic dysfunction that accompany the public's reception of masses of data, so that most people will reluctantly accept its implications as inevitable. One can hope, though, that it, like most New Journalistic publication, will lead to the accomplishment of positive understanding and necessary change. One can hope that with a new consciousness of the world, man can learn and adapt as he must to survive.

6

HOPEFUL SIGNS
AND
CONCLUSIONS

We must place the future, like the unborn
child in the womb of a woman, within a
community of men, women, and children,
among us, already here, already to be
nourished and succored and protected, already
in need of things for which, if they are not
prepared before it is born, it will be too late.
So, as the young say, The Future Is Now.

Margaret Mead in
Culture and Commitment:
A Study of the Generation Gap

In my introduction I spoke of three categories of New
Journalism: the underground press, books and articles by New
Journalists, and changes in the established media. I have considered the first two at length and have yet formally to discuss
the third. It clearly overlaps the second to some extent—as has
been seen, several established publications have presented New
Journalistic material. Also, some changes in the established
media are being influenced by the underground press, for many
conscientious newspapers, for example, have begun to take into
account underground reportage as a valid source of public
information and are, furthermore, being slowly liberalized; and
many underground journalists are now beginning to write for
established papers and magazines, as well as their own. So,
what remains of the task of discussing the third category is a
brief consideration of some other important media changes and
what they imply.

While magazines like *Ramparts, Evergreen Review,* and
Esquire, besides the underground press, have been publishing
various kinds of avant-garde journalism for years, there are

several new magazines that have arisen, many of which I discussed earlier, as well as some established ones that have recently undergone marked change toward the styles and concerns of New Journalism. In the last group I would include *Look*, *Playboy*, the *Atlantic*, and, particularly, *Harper's*. *Harper's* and the *Atlantic* have been responsible for publishing a good deal of New Journalistic work. The changes in *Playboy* and *Look* may be a little more subtle, but they are still to be found if one examines issues over the last three years. While still appealing to some of the most synthetic and crass interests of the American public (I don't mean healthy sex, but sex as a product, women as tools for male pleasure), *Playboy* has nonetheless become a significant platform for some New Journalistic writing—significant partly because of its openness to subject matter and the intelligent journalistic work it publishes and partly because of its large audience. *Look*, under an enlightened editorship, has become one of the most relevant of popular, large-circulation magazines, most obviously since its admirably done issue on the 1970's for 13 January 1970; and it is now publishing a good deal of controversial and somewhat experimental journalism, such as Richard Gooding's "An Exile in My Own Country" (24 February 1970, pp. 19-23), a very honest piece of poetic journalism. Furthermore, there has been a general trend among popular magazines—to a lesser extent among newspapers—to move beyond or challenge the pressure of political and sexual censorship and to exercise more freedom in choosing the kinds of journalism and subject matter to which they will devote themselves.

Newspapers have been traditionally slower than magazines to open themselves to any kind of unconventional or experimental journalism, largely because newspapers have a dominantly local audience which must not be offended lest they go bankrupt from loss of advertising support. Publishers of book-length journalism are the most open of all, because they risk very little, having no set audience and probably a ready one for any book they choose to publish, but most of the journalists whose books they publish have previously written for magazines. So, I think that in the future one can expect to find the development of New Journalistic writing taking place primarily in magazines, both popular—particularly *New York*, which is now Tom Wolfe's major vehicle—and underground; although the underground newspapers should continue to be a seedbed of experiments and a force for breakthroughs in freedom of subject matter, if there are any really significant barriers left to penetrate. Finally, I think, as I said earlier, that the best New Journalistic writing is defining a new genre of literature which is both informational and artistic, and hopefully that genre will develop and find more writers in the near future. It is extremely relevant to the overdue transformation of American culture through a journalistically educated public.

In television journalism there are some significant changes that have occurred in the last few years, although the journalistic potential of television has been tapped only superficially. While many news broadcasts and commentaries seem more numb and cynical than ever about the events they describe and interpret, there are also some good signs to be seen. Television journalism is more and more acting on behalf of the people in criticism of the faults and injustices of American governmental policy, especially in network news shows and in such programs as NBC's *First Tuesday* and CBS's *60 Minutes.* Also, there is available, mostly through special programs, an increasing amount of intelligent information about pollution, urban problems, the Vietnam war, racial conflict, drug culture, and youth, although much reportage of such material frequently has an oversimplified, subtly biased, or hysterical aspect to it. Furthermore, National Educational Television has generally been willing to promote experiments in journalistic broadcasting, especially on such programs as *America, Inc.* On the whole, however, I don't foresee television as a very significant platform for journalism until the advent of cable television, often called "community antenna television" (CATV), which will probably allow the individual broadcaster much more freedom, as well as lower operating costs that will free him from the strangle hold of sponsors.[1]

As far as radio journalism is concerned, the significant changes in the recent past have been implemented (and probably will be in the near future) mainly by underground FM stations, modeled in one degree or another after KMPX and KSAN in San Francisco. AM stations, like local newspapers, are too closely bound to their sponsors and a sensitive general public to open up their programming to experimentation in journalistic practice, and the same holds true for overground

FM. Underground FM survives only where there is a large, hip audience as well as a liberal sponsorship, and at present that means it is an urban phenomenon, predominantly on the east and west coasts, though many stations are now in operation all across the country. There are now several dozen underground FM stations broadcasting on a regular basis, but the fatality rate has been high, largely by reason of financial failure. Nonetheless, where the stations have survived they have been open and creative enough to begin to transform radio journalism and to suggest the tremendous possibilities for its development in the future; and they have experienced virtually no harassment by the FCC, even though they have crossed some touchy language barriers and criticized governmental policy relentlessly. Underground FM is at present probably a more important force for journalistic education than television, though it has a much smaller audience.[2]

All of the developments I have been discussing as part of New Journalism indicate the growth and enrichment of a new consciousness, a larger, more varied, and more complex sense of the immediate human situation. The people participating in the creation of this new consciousness are continuously searching beyond their traditions for new forms of journalistic expression and education; and yet they return to their own cultural environment and its problems and paradoxes to find the raw material of their new message. If Spiro Agnew is concerned about the power of the media, he should be; they have the power to educate the public far beyond what they do now, and New Journalism, in its many forms, is tapping that power as traditional journalism never has—and hopefully for the good of mankind. If it should be pointed out that American journalism is more free from governmental repression than any other in the world, that the New Journalists are somehow abusing that freedom, or that I am being too harsh in my criticism of traditional journalistic practice, I would reply that freedom is the right of man and I am thankful for its preservation, as are the New Journalists, but we can do better than we have in the past in helping the public be creatively aware of the contemporary human universe.

Notes

INTRODUCTION

1. It is important here to distinguish New Journalism from the Precision Journalism practiced by such journalists as Richard Scammon and Ben Wattenberg, authors of the ambitious psephological study of the 1968 elections *The Real Majority: An Extraordinary Examination of the Electorate* (New York, 1970). Scammon and Wattenberg, who consider themselves to be writing in the journalistic style of the future, are related to some of the New Journalists in their exploration of a new "objective" style which involves a combination of Gallup-Poll information, sociological statistics, and polished, descriptive writing. This kind of journalism is undoubtedly becoming increasingly important as an instrument of public education, regardless of its dependence upon the somewhat suspect science of poll-taking and statistical political analysis. (An article which uses methods similar to those of Scammon and Wattenberg and which offers sound critical advice about the limitations of those methods is Philip E. Converse and Howard Schuman's " 'Silent Majorities' and the Vietnam War," *Scientific American*, June 1970, pp. 17-25. I understand also that Philip Meyer of the Knight Newspapers has written an as yet unpublished book on the subject which considers the possibilities of applying the techniques of behavorial science to the writing of Precision Journalism. This experimental journalism should definitely be watched as it develops in the future, and much of it, I am certain, will be welcomed by an aware reading public. However, though it is related to experiments with objectivity in New Journalism, it is not yet really part of the developments I am regarding as New Journalistic. Furthermore, much of it strikes me as being closer to the excesses of abstract data and detached observations of Presidential Commission reports than to the kinds of journalism with which I shall be concerned.

2. "The Press and Its Crisis of Identity" in *Mass Media in a Free Society*, ed. Warren K. Agee (Lawrence: University Press of Kansas, 1969), pp. 9-10. There are a number of informative book-length studies of the government-media relationship. Besides Agee's book, one is especially referred to: *Survey of Broadcast Journalism 1968-1969*, ed. Marvin Barrett (New York: Grosset & Dunlap, Inc., 1969); Herbert I. Schiller, *Mass Communications and the American Empire* (New York: Augustus M. Kelley, 1969); William Small, *To Kill a Messenger: Television News and the Real World* (New York: Hastings House Publishers, Inc., 1970); *The Responsibility of the*

Press, ed. Gerald Gross (New York: Simon and Schuster, 1966); and Dale Minor, *The Information War* (New York: Hawthorn Books, Inc., 1970).

3. From his introduction to *The Black Americans and the Press,* ed. Jack Lyle (Los Angeles: The Ward Ritchie Press, 1968), p. xiii.

4. "The Press and Government: Who's Telling the Truth?" in Agee, pp. 18, 20, 24.

Chapter 1

1. See "Mass Communication, Popular Taste and Organized Social Action" in *Mass Culture: The Popular Arts in America,* ed. Bernard Rosenberg and David Manning White (New York: The Free Press, 1964), pp. 457-473; reprinted from *The Communication of Ideas,* ed. Lyman Bryson (New York: Harper & Brothers, 1948), pp. 95-118.

2. "The Press and Its Crisis of Identity" in *Mass Media in a Free Society,* ed. Warren K. Agee (Lawrence: University Press of Kansas, 1969), pp. 12-13.

3. From the introduction to an anthology of his writings from the *Weekly* entitled *The Haunted Fifties* (New York: Random House, Inc., 1969), p. xviii. Stone also discusses an earlier independent political paper, *In Fact,* edited by the foreign correspondent and liberal crusader George Seldes. He was successful through the 1930's and early 1940's because of left-wing unions, etc., but that support was withdrawn when he backed Tito in his fight with Stalin.

4. *Ibid.,* p. xxi.

5. "un'der·ground, *n.,*" from *Orpheus* (offices in "a roving 1946 Chevrolet school bus"), in *Countdown,* No. 1 (February 1970), p. 176. For some extreme, but well-documented examples of the established press's distorted and uninformative reportage of events involving the Black Panthers of Oakland, California, see Gene Marine's book *The Black Panthers* (New York: New American Library, 1969), pp. 67 ff. For some additional examples with commentary, see Naomi Feigelson, *The Underground Revolution: Hippies, Yippies, and Others* (New York: New American Library, 1970), pp. 114 ff.; and Edward Jay Epstein, "The Panthers and the Police: A Pattern of Genocide?," *New Yorker,* 13 February 1971, pp. 45-77.

6. For a listing see the *Guide to the American Left,* compiled by Laird M. Wilcox, 5th ed. (Kansas City, Mo.: U.S. Directory Service, 1970), which contains also an elaborate bibliography of writings relevant to the press's cultural environment; or see the *Directory of Little Magazines and Small Presses,* ed. Len Fulton, 5th ed. (Paradise, Calif.: Dust Books, 1969). Also, the underground magazine *Countdown,* No. 1 (February 1970), published an up-to-date list of UPS members. The most comprehensive list is to be found in Robert Glessing's

The Underground Press in America (Bloomington and London: Indiana University Press, 1970), pp. 178-90. Glessing's book is an excellent historical guide to the underground press and is founded on a wealth of factual information. Glessing is an experienced editor and publisher and is also a teacher of journalism at Cañada College in Redwood City, California.

7. Quoted from Jacob Brackman, "The Underground Press," *Playboy,* August 1967, p. 96.
8. *Ibid.,* p. 152.
9. *Ibid.,* p. 151.
10. *Ibid.,* p. 151.
11. (Harrisburg, Pa.: Stackpole Books, 1970), pp. 25, 27. Romm prefers to call the presses "street-corner," a kind of journalism with roots in prerevolutionary America (Peter Zenger's early eighteenth-century New York paper, the *Weekly Journal,* is an example). The adjective *underground* for her connotes the "anti-Fascist resistance press of Europe," like *L'Italia Libera,* which a man risked his life to read (see pp. 18-19). Despite harassment, the American "underground" papers are more available than that, and her argument is sound. Nonetheless, the name has stuck, and I will use it with its newer set of connotations. Her book is a valuable collection of underground fragments, as well as a good commentary on the presses and their culture. There are several other anthologies which are good, representative collections of the underground's journalistic work: *The Hippie Papers,* ed. Jerry Hopkins (New York: New America Library, 1967); *Notes from the New Underground,* ed. Jesse Kornbluth (New York: Ace Publishing Corp., 1968); *The Movement toward a New America: The Beginnings of a Long Revolution,* ed. Mitchell Goodman (New York: Random House, Inc., 1970); *Fire!: Reports from the Underground Press,* ed. Paul Samberg (New York: E. P. Dutton & Co., Inc., 1970); and the *Underground Press Digest,* published bimonthly from New York by Robert Farrell.
12. "Underground Alliance," *Time,* 29 July 1966, p. 57.
13. Romm, pp. 27, 29.
14. The "obscenity busts" are usually really political, motivated by local reaction to a paper's dissent. Complaint about this fact is to be found frequently in underground papers. For a rundown on these busts across the country during the last few years, see *Orpheus*-editor Thomas Forcade's article "Obscene Scene," *Countdown,* No. 2, pp. 186-166 (the magazine numbers pages backwards). The most articulate plea for a total change in pornography laws so that they can't be used as political levers to suppress dissent was made by Art Kunkin, editor of the Los Angeles *Free Press,* before the President's Commission on Obscenity and Pornography, which met with him at the Los Angeles City Hall, 4 May 1970. The statement, printed in

the *Free Press,* 22 May 1970, p. 6, received little official press attention, however, because Tom Forcade of UPS threw a pie in the face of one of the commissioners—an event worth recording, to be sure, but not at the expense of Kunkin's genuinely concerned plea, which the official press virtually ignored.

15. Quoted from Romm, p. 27.
16. "Underground Alliance," p. 57.
17. Quoted in Brackman, p. 154.
18. *Ibid.,* p. 155.
19. LNS is now located in New York, and Mungo is still writing a vibrant New Journalism. See, particularly, his article "If Mr. Thoreau Calls, Tell Him I've Left the Country," an account of the commune's life and the now polluted rivers and country of Thoreau, in the *Atlantic,* May 1970, pp. 72-85. The article is a good example of New Journalism and of the influence of the underground on the subject matter of a more traditional magazine. More recently Mungo has published a book on the farm and related topics entitled *Total Loss Farm: A Year in the Life* (New York: E. P. Dutton & Co., Inc., 1970).
20. Raymond Mungo, *Famous Long Ago: My Life and Hard Times with Liberation News Service* (Boston: Beacon Press, 1970).

Chapter 2

1. *The Open Conspiracy: What America's Angry Generation Is Saying* (Harrisburg, Pa.: Stackpole Books, 1970), pp. 23, 25.
2. Quoted from *ibid.,* p. 25.
3. *Revolutionary Notes* (New York: Grove Press, Inc., 1969), pp. 52-53.
4. See, for instance, Gene Marine's account in *The Black Panthers* (New York: New American Library, 1969), pp. 114-15, of the *Movement's* supporting Eldridge Cleaver when he was campaigning to be a U.S. presidential candidate.
5. The black press in America has always been a weak journalistic organ, for a number of reasons, largely obvious ones. The most powerful black newspapers of the recent past were the Pittsburgh *Courier* and the Washington *Afro-American.* Since their decline there are still some relatively influential papers, like the New York *Age* and the Chicago *Defender,* but there are very few dailies. Chuck Stone, who edited and wrote columns for all of these except the *Courier,* at one time or another, has collected together some of his best columns in a book called *Tell It Like It Is* (New York: Pocket Books, 1968). The columns were written in the early 1960's and represent one of the important beginnings of black power in journalism, even though they seem pretty mild now. Stone wrote incisively and eloquently. At San Francisco, in April of 1964, he gave the keynote address at the National Newspaper Publishers' Convention. In that address, printed in

his book, pp. 75-78, he called for a new vitality, pride, pursuit of power, and relevance in black journalism—an end which underground papers, black and otherwise, have realized more fully than the established black press.

6. (New York: Avon Books, 1969), p. xi of her introduction. Besides Divoky's book there is another good anthology entitled *Our Time Is Now: Notes from the High School Underground,* ed. John Birmingham (New York, Washington, and London: Frederick A. Praeger, Inc., 1970), which includes a helpful context-defining introduction by Kurt Vonnegut.

7. Quoted from Divoky, pp. 146-47. The underground press, of high schools and otherwise, continuously criticizes American educational institutions, most of the time justly. It has been responsible in part for the growing awareness of the need for educational reform and has helped spawn a new educational journalism, the best of it to be found in publications like *This Magazine Is About Schools,* published quarterly in Toronto, whose concerns and style are frequently close to those of publications of the underground.

8. Divoky, p. 169. See also the New York *Times,* 9 May 1969, which features a report on high-school unrest in the city.

9. Quoted from Jacob Brackman, "The Underground Press," *Playboy* August 1967, p. 151.

10. *Ibid.,* p. 152.

11. "un'der·ground, *n.*," *Countdown,* No. 1, pp. 180-178 (numbered backwards).

12. See Brackman, pp. 155-56.

13. *Famous Long Ago: My Life and Hard Times with Liberation News Service* (Boston: Beacon Press, 1970), p. 187.

14. *Ibid.,* p. 201. Ethel Romm includes in her book, previously cited, a short appendix (pp. 250-51) which contains a wealth of brief information about the underground press, some of which I would like to borrow here in order to supplement the bibliographical data I have noted in the last two chapters. The best collections of underground newspapers are at the State Historical Society of Wisconsin at Madison and the Department of Library Science at the University of Michigan at Ann Arbor. Other collections are to be found at the Stanford University Library, Stanford, California; University of Colorado Libraries, Boulder, Colorado; Bucknell University Library, Lewisburg, Pennsylvania; Prince George's County Memorial Library, Hyattsville, Maryland; Long Island University Library, Brookville, New York; Iowa City Public Library, Iowa City, Iowa; Department of Anthropology and Sociology, University of British Columbia, Vancouver, Canada; and Kent State University Library, Kent, Ohio. Many other libraries offer more limited collections. With Romm, I would recommend the "Magazines" column in *Library Journal* for good evaluative

criticism of some of the underground-press publications. There are also several books on the underground press and related topics which she lists as now in preparation: "A history with documents of the New Left, ed. by Massimo Teodori, Bobbs Merrill; a book on the Movement and the *Rat*, by its editor Jeff Shero, Random House; the 2nd edition of *From Radical Left to Extreme Right, Current Periodicals of Protest, Controversy or Dissent—USA*, ed. by Dr. R. H. Muller and T. Spahn, Dept. of Library Science, U. of Mich. . . .; *Something's Happening*, by Richard Neville, ed. and pub. of OZ, a London member of UPS, McGraw Hill." She also lists two anthologies of earlier New Left writing which might be of interest: *The New Student Left*, ed. Mitchell Cohen and Dennis Hale (Boston: Beacon Press, 1966); and *The New Radicals*, ed. Paul Jacobs and Saul Landau (New York: Random House, Inc., 1966). Further lists of related materials may be found in the *Guide to the American Left*, compiled by Laird M. Wilcox, 5th ed. (Kansas City, Mo.: U.S. Directory Service, 1970).

Chapter 3

1. (New York: Random House, Inc., 1965), p. 3.

2. Talese is an immensely talented journalist, although he is not a New Journalist in quite the same ways that Wolfe, Capote, or other writers I am discussing are. Although he is committed to accurate and artistic journalism with more than tentative historical value, he is less personal than many New Journalists and is more old-fashioned in his style and interests than most of them are—although his portraits of personalities for *Esquire* and other magazines (collected in *Fame and Obscurity* [New York: World Publishing Co., 1970]) show him taking a more New Journalistic tack. I have no doubt, however, that Wolfe learned a great deal from him. His book *The Bridge* (New York: Harper & Row Publishers, 1964), about the building of the Verrazano-Narrows Bridge linking Brooklyn to Staten Island, is something of a landmark in journalistic writing about the projects of modern metropolitan architecture and engineering. His massive and intricately researched history of the New York *Times, The Kingdom and the Power* (New York: World Publishing Co., 1969), is the last word on how the greatest established newspaper in the world grew to its present position of tremendous, if somewhat waning, power over public knowledge and opinion. This unauthorized journalistic history, derived from hundreds of interviews with *Times* people as well as from family albums and personal files, suggests Talese's affinity with Theodore White and William Manchester on the one hand and —insofar as he is writing as a nonfiction novelist—with Truman Capote on the other. However, as good a writer as Talese is as an

institutional historian and as a narrator of the psychologies of real people, he is not as innovative a stylist as are many New Journalists—including Capote, in my opinion—and *The Kingdom and the Power*, as literary art, is perhaps closer to Arthur Hailey's *Airport* or *Hotel* than to Capote's *In Cold Blood*. Nonetheless, it is a valuable book for anyone interested in modern journalism—it is probably the best book ever written about the established press—and it has an elaborate and useful index.

3. (New York: Pocket Books, 1966), pp. xi-xii. This paperback edition is from that of Farrar, Straus & Giroux (New York, 1965). Further quotations from this edition are cited by page number in the text.

4. I will be citing quotations by page number from the Bantam Books (Toronto, New York, London: 1969) editions of these books. They were both published originally by Farrar, Straus & Giroux (New York: 1968). Because these two books are adequately representative of Wolfe's development, I am omitting discussion of his more recent work, *Radical Chic and Mau-Mauing the Flak Catchers* (New York: Farrar, Straus & Giroux, Inc., 1970).

5. "Double Perspective on Hysteria," *Saturday Review,* 24 August 1968, p. 37. Although he is "close to the hippies and acid heads" in some ways, Wolfe does not, I understand, approve of their use of drugs.

6. (New York: New American Library, 1968), p. 99. Further quotations from this New American Library paperback edition will be cited by page number in the text.

7. (New York, 1968), p. 56. Further quotations from this New American Library paperback edition will be cited by page number in the text.

8. "The Conventions, 1968," *Commentary,* December 1968, p. 93.

9. From a paper read at the Modern Language Association meeting and published in *Commentary,* March 1966, pp. 39 ff. I am quoting here from Robert Langbaum's essay "Mailer's New Style" in his book *The Modern Spirit: Essays on the Continuity of Nineteenth- and Twentieth-Century Literature* (New York: Oxford University Press, 1970), p. 148. Langbaum is helpful with the novels, but he is only briefly concerned with Mailer's journalism.

10. Pp. 24-41, 51-63, and 57-74, respectively. I will cite quotations by page number in the text. These articles, with additional material, have been incorporated into Mailer's recent book *Of a Fire on the Moon* (Boston: Little, Brown & Co., 1970), the end product of the *Life* contract.

11. There are few books about scientific endeavor that are really well written. Mailer's work on the astronauts thus helps to fill a gap and also to bridge some of the points of separation of C. P. Snow's "two cultures," science and humanism. Another scientific book which is written very largely as a kind of personal journalism is *The Double Helix* (New York: Atheneum Publishers, 1968), Nobel Prize-winner

James D. Watson's account of the people and events surrounding the discovery of the structure of DNA. Watson's book is only somewhat obliquely a part of the New Journalism, but it is pretty well written and, like Mailer's, portrays the human situations behind what seem on the surface to be accomplished, cold events.

Chapter 4

1. *The World of Jimmy Breslin,* a selection of Breslin's writing annotated by James G. Bellows and Richard C. Wald (New York: Ballantine Books, Inc., 1969), pp. 152, 153.
2. There are two good earlier book-length, personal-journalistic accounts of visits to North Vietnam: Harrison Salisbury's *Behind the Lines— Hanoi* (New York: Harper & Row Publishers, 1966), which was first published in parts in the New York *Times* during his visit in 1965-66; and Staughton Lynd and Tom Hayden's *The Other Side* (New York: New American Library, 1967), an antiwar-movement report.
3. Quoted from the account reprinted in her *Styles of Radical Will* (New York: Dell Publishing Co., Inc., 1970), pp. 205-6. Further quotations will be cited by page number in the text.
4. (Toronto, New York, London: Bantam Books, 1968), pp. 25-26, 27. Further quotations from this Bantam paperback edition will be cited by page number in the text. Excerpts from Wakefield's book appeared in the *Atlantic,* March 1968, pp. 39-54.
5. (New York: Dell Publishing Co., Inc., 1969), pp. 3-4. This Delta (Dell Publishing Co.) paperback edition is from that of Farrar, Straus & Giroux (New York, 1968). Further quotations from this edition will be cited by page number in the text.
6. (New York: Ace Publishing Corp., 1970), pp. 11-12. Further quotations will be cited by page number in the text.
7. There are two other books on ghetto schools that I would recommend as good examples of New Journalism: Herbert Kohl's *36 Children* (New York: New American Library, 1967), which is about a Harlem school; and James Herndon's *The Way It Spozed to Be* (New York: Simon & Schuster, 1968). Another more recent book in a similar style with related concerns is Henry S. Resnick's *Turning On the System* (New York: Pantheon Publishers, 1970), which is about the attempt and subsequent failure to reform the Philadelphia Public School system.
8. (Toronto, New York, and London: Bantam Books, 1967), p. xi. Further quotations from this Bantam paperback edition will be cited by page number in the text.
9. (Toronto, New York, and London: Bantam Books, 1968), p. 24. Further quotations will be cited by page number in the text. Two other books that may be compared in technique to Hersey's are Jessica

Mitford's *The Trial of Doctor Spock* (New York: Alfred A. Knopf, Inc., 1969), a "re-creation" of Spock's trial for encouraging avoidance of the draft, and *The Tales of Hoffman*, eds. Mark L. Levine, George C. McNamee, and Daniel Greenberg (Toronto, New York, and London: Bantam Books, 1970), which is an edited transcript of the trial of the "Chicago 8." There are many books now in print concerned with the urban riots. One which I would recommend, both as an example of this kind of New Journalism and as a reasonably objective account, is *Rebellion in Newark: Official Violence and Ghetto Response* (New York: Random House, Inc., 1967), by Tom Hayden, a New Leftist and an SDS leader, who was a community organizer in Newark.

10. (New York: New American Library, 1969), pp. 9, 10.

11. Another book concerned with racial conflict which reflects New Journalistic influence is *The Second Civil War: Arming for Armageddon* (New York: New American Library, 1968), by Garry Wills, who bases his report on information gathered from interviews and observations during an extended tour of the United States. Two recent articles, among others, exemplify the writing style of and the historical awareness of racial problems on the part of New Journalists: Larry King's "Confessions of a White Racist," *Harper's*, January 1970, pp. 63-77, and *Harper's* former Editor-in-Chief Willie Morris' "Yazoo . . . Notes on Survival," *Harper's*, June 1970, pp. 43-70.

12. (New York: Random House, Inc., 1970), pp. xi-xii. Further quotations will be cited by page number in the text. Some 30,000 words of *My Lai 4* were published in *Harper's*, May 1970, pp. 53-84. Incidentally, since Hersh's book raises questions about the relations of the press and the courts, there is a book on the subject: *Justice and the Press* (Boston: Beacon Press, 1966), by John Lofton, an associate editor of the Pittsburgh *Post-Gazette*.

13. Besides Hersh's book on the My Lai 4 massacre, there is *One Morning in the War* (New York: Coward McCann, Inc., 1970), by Richard Hammer, a New York *Times* reporter, which might be helpful, in a comparison, as a way of checking the accuracy of Hersh's work. There is a great deal of exposé journalism concerning Vietnam, as one might suspect. An interesting example, partly a New Journalistic nonfiction short story reminiscent of Capote's *In Cold Blood* and partly a record of interrogation and aftermath, is Normand Poirer's "An American Atrocity," *Esquire*, August 1969, pp. 59 ff., which concerns U.S. Marine atrocities in Xuan Ngoc on 23 September 1966. There is also a critical and imaginative New Journalistic account of the training and stateside life of Green Berets entitled "Lt. Troll," *US*, No. 3 (May 1970), pp. 5-28, by Toby Thompson, who writes frequently for *US* and the *Village Voice*. Thompson's article is relevant to any attempt to comprehend the war. There are a number of

books and articles which could be discussed under the first heading of "The General Scene," but I would like to note a few that exemplify some of the reach of New Journalistic writing: *The Day of St. Anthony's Fire* (New York: Macmillan Co., 1968), a reconstruction of the ergot-fungus poisoning (which has the effects of LSD) of the inhabitants of the French village Pont-Saint-Esprit, by John G. Fuller, author of *Incident at Exeter*, who visited the village and talked extensively with its people; *The New Indians* (New York: Dell Publishing Co., 1968), an informed exposé and intelligent discussion of the plight of reservation Indians, by Stan Steiner, who lived among the tribes; *Paper Lion* (New York: Harper & Row Publishers, 1966), by George Plimpton, who lived and worked out with the Detroit Lions in order to write this intimate, humorous, and revealing book about professional football, and who has written similar books on other sports; the account of Senator Eugene McCarthy's campaign, "Nobody Knows . . . Reflections on the McCarthy Campaign: Part I" and "————: Part II," *Harper's*, April 1969, pp. 62-80, and May 1969, pp. 71-94, respectively, by Jeremy Larner, a novelist and McCarthy's main speech-writer; "Charley Starkweather: Wheel on Fire," *US*, No. 1 (June 1969), pp. 22-35, an account of "1958's crazy-mixed-up Nebraska teenage killer," by Michael Lydon, an erstwhile *Newsweek* reporter whose writing on rock culture and other subjects has appeared in *Esquire, Rolling Stone,* and the now defunct mod-culture magazine, *Eye*; "The Most Unforgettable Character I Never Met," *US*, No. 3 (May 1970), pp. 45-59, an imaginative and humorous account of the rise of Billy Graham, by Richard Goldstein, a rock critic, journalist, and editor of *US*; and "Twirling at Ole Miss," *Esquire*, February 1963, pp. 100 ff., a black-humor report on the incredible Dixie National Baton Twirling Institute, by novelist-screenwriter Terry Southern.

Chapter 5

1. A book which bears useful comparison with Draper's is *The Berkeley Student Revolt: Facts and Interpretations*, eds. S. M. Lipset and S. S. Wolin (New York: Doubleday & Co., Inc., 1966). Besides Draper's book and the ones I will be discussing, I would recommend, both as examples of this new kind of journalism and as helpful background: *It's Happening* (Santa Barbara: Marc-Laird Publications, 1966), a very readable and generally informative book of psychosociological journalism, by J. L. Simmons, a sociologist, and Barry Winograd, a teacher and journalist; *The Whole World Is Watching: A Young Man Looks at Youth's Dissent* (New York: Paperback Library, 1970), a book comparable to *It's Happening,* though baggier and more self-serious, and written from a younger intelligence, by

Mark Gerzon; *The Gap* (New York: New American Library, 1969), an account of the interactions of two generations, by Richard Lorber and Ernest Fladell; *Confrontation on Campus: Student Challenge in California* (Los Angeles: Ward Ritchie Press, 1969), by Art Seidenbaum, with some excellent photography by Bill Bridges; *Is the Library Burning?* (New York: Random House, Inc., 1969), a tour of campuses where student activism and rebellion have occurred, by Roger Rapoport and Lawrence J. Kirshbaum; *The Student Revolution: A Global Confrontation* (New York: W. W. Norton & Co., Inc., 1970), by Joseph A. Califano, who was previously a special assistant to President Johnson and traveled to every center of student activism in the world to write this moderate and intelligent report; *Long March, Short Spring: The Student Uprising at Home and Abroad* (New York and London: Monthly Review Press, 1969), a book comparable to Califano's, by Barbara and John Ehrenreich; "The Baptism of Brandeis U.," *US*, No. 1 (June 1969), pp. 69-92, a portrait of black and radical activism on a Jewish campus, by Jon Landau, a student there as well as a rock critic for *Rolling Stone* and *Crawdaddy*. There are two recent books concerning the increasing militance and violence involved in student activism: *Push Comes to Shove: The Escalation of Student Protest* (Boston: Houghton, Mifflin Co., 1970), a report on the goals and contradictions of the escalation, by Steven Kelman; *The Middle of the Country* (New York: Avon Books, 1970), a quickie anthology of accounts of the Kent State killings of 4 May 1970, by students and faculty of the university, ed. Bill Warren, a Kent State student.

2. (New York: Avon Books, 1970), pp. 9, 12-13. The original Random House edition was published in 1969. Further quotations from the paperback edition will be cited by page number in the text. Kunen has also written an irreverent, hip account of the Apollo 11 flight, "The Great Rocketship," *US*, No. 1 (June 1969), pp. 11-20, which makes an interesting generation-gap comparison with Mailer's *Of a Fire on the Moon*. A book which is helpful in understanding the events at Columbia of which Kunen and Rader write is *Up Against the Ivy Wall: A History of the Columbia Crisis* (New York: Atheneum Publishers, 1968), by Jerry Avorn, *et al.*

3. (New York: Paperback Library, 1969), pp. 35-36.

4. *The Jefferson Airplane and the San Francisco Sound* (New York: Ballantine Books, Inc., 1969), pp. 47, 48-49.

5. There are many good article-length pieces of rock journalism that have not been anthologized. Two recent ones which strike me as especially significant examples of New Journalism are: Michael Lydon, "The Rolling Stones—at Play in the Apocalypse," *Ramparts*, March 1970, pp. 26-53, the best account on the Stones of which I know; and Toby Thompson, "Hey Hey Woody Guthrie Ah Wrote

Yew a Song," *US*, No. 2 (October 1969), pp. 16-33, a personal and creative account of Bob Dylan's boyhood environment in Hibbing, Minnesota. Thompson is presently working on a book on Dylan. Richard Goldstein, the editor of *US*, is himself an important rock critic and New Journalist who writes for the *Village Voice, Vogue, Life,* and many other magazines, and lectured on New Journalism at Columbia University in the spring of 1969.

6. (New York: Ballantine Books, Inc., 1967), pp. 51-52. Further quotations from this Ballantine paperback edition will be by page number in the text.

7. There is a wealth of journalism more sympathetic to Haight-Ashbury than Von Hoffman's—in the underground press, for instance—but much of it is not so well-informed and clear-eyed as his. One of the most intelligent, sympathetic books is *The Hippie Trip* (New York: Pegasus, 1968), a personal but sociologically oriented account of the California scene, by sociologist Lewis Yablonsky, who previously wrote *The Violent Gang* (New York: Penguin Books, Inc., 1966), in which he reports his experiences with urban street gangs, and *The Tunnel Back: Synanon* (New York: Macmillan Co., 1965), an account of Synanon's activities in rehabilitating drug-users. A good, very sympathetic anthology is *Voices from the Love Generation,* ed. L. Wolf (Boston: Little, Brown & Co., 1968). Or, for two articles close to Von Hoffman's skeptical side, see: Anthony Lukas, "The Life and Death of a Hippie," *Esquire,* May 1968, pp. 106 ff., an account dealing with the murders of James "Groovy" Hutchinson and Linda Fitzpatrick in a Greenwich Village basement; and Joan Didion, "Slouching Towards Bethlehem," in her book of the same title (New York, 1969) discussed in the previous chapter.

8. (New York: Fawcett Publications, Inc., 1969), p. 9. Further quotations from this Fawcett paperback edition will be cited by page number in the text.

9. (New York: Doubleday & Co., Inc., 1970), p. 11. Another recent book which qualifies to some extent as autobiographical journalism is Frank Conroy's *Stop-Time* (New York: Dell Publishing Co., Inc., 1969), a brilliant novel about growing up in the last two decades.

10. Her articles for the *Voice* are collected in a book called *Off Washington Square,* which is now out of print.

11. (New York: Random House, Inc., 1970), p. 179. Further quotations from this Vintage paperback will be cited by page number in the text.

12. (New York: New American Library, 1970), pp. viii, xiii-xiv, xvi. Two other books with a journalistic bias concerning turned-on culture, which exemplify the range of such work, are: *LSD on Campus* (New York: Dell Publishing Co., Inc., 1966), one of the first attempts to report on and document the role of LSD in American society, by Warren R. Young, a former science editor of *Life,* and Joseph R.

Hixson, a former science editor of *Newsweek;* and *The Teachings of Don Juan: A Yaqui Way of Knowledge* (New York: Ballantine Books, Inc., 1969), a fascinating story of an anthropology graduate student's experiences over five years with a Yaqui Indian shaman, peyote, and various organic religious drugs, by Carlos Castaneda. The best periodical publication devoted to drug culture was the *Psychedelic Review,* begun in 1966 and edited by Ralph Metzner, Timothy Leary, *et al.,* distributed bimonthly, until defunct, by the Head Shop in New York City. For a scary and well-written account of how drug laws are used as tools of political manipulation, see Leslie Fiedler's very personal and somewhat New Journalistic *Being Busted* (New York: Stein and Day, 1969), which is also, in passing, a good collection of examples of the established press's ineptitude and injustice, which the book attempts, in part, to correct.

13. There is a wealth of writing about the Chicago convention riots, but a good collection of representative reportage and commentary is *Telling It Like It Was: The Chicago Riots,* ed. Walter Schneir (New York: New American Library, 1969), which contains writing by Richard Goldstein, Tom Hayden, Jimmy Breslin, and others. Also a good run-down on the conspiracy trial which followed may be found in Nicholas von Hoffman's "The Chicago Conspiracy Circus," *Playboy,* June 1970, pp. 87 ff., or in Jason Epstein's *The Great Conspiracy Trial* (New York: Random House, Inc., 1970). One aspect of the radical scene with which I haven't dealt, largely because there is little good journalism associated with it, is Women's Liberation. There is clearly a growing journalistic interest in the movement, but it hasn't yet begun to come to fruition. Though there are several books on Women's Liberation now available (Kate Millett's *Sexual Politics* [New York: Doubleday & Co., Inc., 1970] being the best, or at least most stimulating, in my opinion), they are generally more historical and explanatory than journalistic. Julie Ellis' *Revolt of the Second Sex* (New York: Lancer Books, 1970), a history and survey of the present scene, is the only one I know of that is very journalistic, and it is a rather exploitive, impersonal book. Some of the best magazine journalism on the movement is to be found in a double issue of *Motive,* Nos. 6 and 7 (March-April 1969), entitled *On the Liberation of Women.* There are also pieces in the underground press more frequently now, and in the popular press as well, but the major New Journalism of Women's Liberation will probably come later in the 1970's.

Chapter 6

1. For a thorough report on the possibilities of CATV, see Ralph Lee Smith, "The Wired Nation," *Nation,* 18 May 1970, a special issue

devoted to his report. A brief but direct indictment of network television for failing to be publicly informative is FCC Commissioner Nicholas Johnson's "The Wasteland Revisited," *Playboy*, December 1970, pp. 229 ff.

2. It will undoubtedly occur to some people that movies are also, occasionally, a kind of journalism and that I have neglected them in my discussion. Indeed, I think they are, though in a way different from that of the media I have been considering, but that is an involved idea which would itself require a book for proper treatment. A good, though now somewhat out-of-date anthology of ideas about the social effects of all the media, including movies, is *Mass Communication*, ed. Wilbur Schramm (Urbana: University of Illinois Press, 1960). A comparable but more up-to-date book—and one unified by a continuous point of view—is Ben H. Bagdikian's *The Information Machines: Their Impact on Men and the Media* (New York: Harper & Row Publishers, 1971).

Index

Aardvark, 9

Abernathy, Rev. Ralph, 82

Adams, Henry, 80

Adler, Ruth, 46

Agee, James, 87

Age of Rock: Sounds of the American Cultural Revolution, The, 129–30

Akwesasne Notes, 30

Aldrin, Buzz, 82

Algiers Motel Incident, The, 102, 103, 106–109

Allen Ginsberg in America, 134, 137–39

Alternative: Communal Life in New America, The, 142

America, Inc., xvi, 151

American Revelation, 36

Amistad: Writings on Black History and Culture, 29

Anderson, Chester, 31

Ankh, 33

Armies of the Night, The, 58, 64–70

Armstrong, Neil, 82

Arnoni, M. F., 9

Atlantic, xvi, 103, 122, 150

Avant Garde, 37, 38

Avatar, xvi, 15, 20, 25, 39

Bagdikian, Ben H., xiii, 4

Barb, 16, 17, 28

Beatitude, 14

Beatles, The, 129

Being Busted, 165n12

Be Not Content, 134, 136–37

Berkeley: The New Student Revolt, 120

Big Ass, 32

Black Panther, 28

Black Panthers, The, xvi, 102, 109–12, 131, 154n5, 156n4

Bloom, Marshall, 19

Boston *Globe,* 103

Bowart, Walter, 16, 19

Brackman, Jacob, 9, 12, 28, 32, 37, 40

Breslin, Jimmy, 83, 89–90

Bridge, The, 158n2

Cannibals and Christians, 64

Capote, Truman, 47, 48–50, 58, 63, 64, 83, 87, 88, 97, 109, 113, 159n2, 161n13

Céline, Ferdinand, 55, 56

Cheetah, 130

Cleaver, Eldridge, 28, 29, 70, 110, 156n4

Closed Corporation, The, 88, 145

Cobb, Ron, 13

Cohen, Allen, 19

cold-type offset printing, 14–15

Collins, Michael, 82

Columbia *Spectator,* 123

Combustion, 14

Communication Company, The, 40

Conroy, Frank, 164n9

CORE (Congress of Racial Equality), 12

Countdown, 37, 38, 39, 142, 154n6

Craddock, William J., 134, 136–37

Crawdaddy, 31, 129, 130

Cronkite, Walter, 20

Daily Californian, 31, 128

Davies, Hunter, 129

Dear Doctor Hip Pocrates: Advice Your Family Doctor Never Gave You, 18

Death at an Early Age: The Destruction of the Hearts and Minds of Negro Children in the Boston Public Schools, 102, 103–106

Detroit *Free Press,* 106

Didion, Joan, 96–100

Diggers, 30, 40

Directory of Little Magazines and Small Presses, 154n6

Division Street: America, 96

Divoky, Diane, 33–34

Do It!, 119, 143

Double Helix, The, 159–60n11

Draper, Hal, 120

Earth Times, 30, 31

East Village Other, xvi, 15, 16–17, 19, 32, 35, 45

Ebony, 28

Education of Henry Adams, The, 80

Ehrlich, Paul, 145

Eisen, Jonathan, 130

Electric Kool-Aid Acid Test, The, 54, 58–62

Ellison, Harlan, 100–102

Ellison, Ralph, 107

El Malcriado, 29

Environment, 30

Esquire, 51, 52, 64, 90, 149, 158n2

Evergreen Review, 149

Fame and Obscurity, 158n2

Famous Long Ago: My Life and Hard Times with Liberation News Service, 19–22

Fancher, Ed, 7

Farber, Jerry, 121

Fiedler, Leslie, 165n12

Fifth Estate, 16, 18

First Tuesday, xvi, 102, 151

Forcade, Thomas, 155–56n14

Fruitcup, 37, 39

Fuck You: A Magazine of the Arts, 37

Gargoyle, 37

Ginsberg, Allen, 39, 77

Ginzburg, Ralph, 38

GI underground press, 32

Glass Teat, The, 100–102

Gleason, Ralph, 127, 129, 130

Glessing, Robert, 154–55n6

Goldstein, Richard, 9, 38, 164n5

Gothic Blimp Works, 32

Great Speckled Bird, 18

Green Revolution, 30, 31

Grell, Jon, 35–36

Guardian, 26, 27, 28

Guide to the American Left, 154n6, 158n14

Gustaitis, Rasa, 134, 139–42

Hard Times, 145

Hard Times: An Oral History of the Great Depression, 96

Harper's, xvi, 64, 150

Harrington, Michael, 9

Hayden, Tom, 145, 160n2, 161n9

Hecht, Ben, 50

Hedgepeth, William, 142

Hell's Angels: A Strange and Terrible Saga, 131–33

Hemingway, Ernest, 50, 72, 78, 79, 89

Hentoff, Nat, 9, 130

Hersey, John, 47, 83, 87, 88, 102, 103, 106–109, 110, 113

Hersh, Seymour M., 102, 103, 112–15

High School Independent Press Service (HIPS), 35

Hiroshima, 47, 87, 109

History of the Standard Oil Company, 87

Hoffman, Abbie, 39, 77, 143–44

Hopkins, Jerry, 129

Horseshit, 9

How Old Will You Be in 1984?: Expressions of Student Outrage from the High School Free Press, 33–34

Hughes, Howard, 99–100

Hughes, Langston, 105–106

I Ain't Marchin' Anymore, 121, 124–26
I. F. Stone's Weekly, 4–5, 7, 9
In Cold Blood, 47, 48–50, 58, 97, 109, 159n2, 161n13
Independent, The, 9
In Fact, 154n3

Jackson State, 40
Jefferson Airplane and the San Francisco Sound, The, 129
Johnson, Lyndon B., 11, 12, 76, 120
Jungle, The, 47, 87

Kandy-Kolored Tangerine-Flake Streamline Baby, xvi, 48, 51–54, 55
Katzman, Allan, 15, 16
Katzman, Don, 15
Keating, Brian, 20
Kennedy, John F., 10, 11, 12, 14, 46, 64
Kent State, 40
Kerouac, Jack, 58
Kesey, Ken, 30, 54, 59–61, 142
Kindman, Michael, 18
Kingdom and the Power, The, 158–59n2
Kiss, 32
Kopkind, Andrew, 145
Kozol, Jonathan, 102, 103–106, 110
Kramer, Jane, 134, 137–39
Krassner, Paul, 9, 10, 14
Kunen, James, xvi, 87, 88, 121–24, 125
Kunkin, Art, 13, 155–56n14

Landau, Jon, 130
Lardner, Ring, 50, 89
Lazarsfeld, Paul F., 3, 95
Lester, Julius, 27–28
Let Us Now Praise Famous Men, 87
Lewis, Oscar, 96

Liberation News Service (LNS), 5, 6, 19–21, 29, 38, 41, 142
Life, 47, 72, 79, 115
Look, 150
Los Angeles *Free Press,* xvi, 13–18 *passim,* 28, 30, 100, 102, 121
Lowell, Robert, 65
Lydon, Michael, 128
Lyle, Jack, xiv
Lynd, Staughton, 26

McGinnis, Joe, 88, 145
McLuhan, Marshall, xii, xiii, 6, 25, 45, 55
Mad, 9, 10
Mailer, Norman, xi, xvi, 7, 8, 10, 50, 58, 62–83, 87–91 *passim,* 99, 106, 124, 143, 159n10, 159–60n11, 163n2
Making of a Counter Culture: Reflections on the Technocratic Society and Its Youthful Opposition, The, 11
Marcus, Greil, 130
Marine, Gene, xvi, 102, 103, 109–12, 131, 134, 135, 154n5, 156n4
Mayday, 145
Melville, Herman, 71, 82
Merry Pranksters, 30, 54, 59–61, 142
Merton, Robert K., 3, 95
Miami and the Siege of Chicago: An Informal History of the Republican and Democratic Conventions of 1968, xvi, 70–79
Minority of One, 9
Mississippi Notebook, 134
Monocle, 9
Movement, 26, 28, 156n4
Moyers, Bill, xiv
Muhammad Speaks, 28
Mungo, Raymond, 19–22, 41, 47, 58, 75, 142, 156n19

My Lai 4: A Report on the Massacre and Its Aftermath, 102, 103, 112–15

Nader, Ralph, 144, 145
Navasky, Victor, 9
New Journalism, definition of, xv
New Muckrakers, definition of, 144
Newton, Huey, 28
New York, 54–55, 122, 150
New York *Free Press,* 33
New York *Herald Tribune,* xvi, 51, 52, 89, 131
New York High School Free Press, 36
New York *Review of Sex,* 33
New York *Times,* 31, 35, 39, 45, 46, 70, 77, 128, 131, 132, 158n2
North Carolina Anvil, 18

Oakland *Tribune,* 28
Of a Fire on the Moon, 72, 143, 159n10, 163n2
One Flew Over the Cuckoo's Nest, 59
On the Road, 58
Open Conspiracy: What America's Angry Generation Is Saying, The, 12–13
Open Door, 36
Oracle. See San Francisco *Oracle*
Ovshinsky, Harvey, 18

Paper, 16, 18
Penthouse, 33
Pittsburgh *Courier,* 156n5
Playboy, 33, 150
Pleasure, 32
Poirer, Richard, 130
Population Bomb, The, 145
Precision Journalism, 153n1
Presidential Papers of Norman Mailer, The, 64
Progressive, 103

Pump House Gang, The, 54, 55–58, 62
Rader, Dotson, 121, 124–26
Ramparts, xvi, 109, 128, 130, 149
Rat, 33, 35, 39
Realist, The, 9, 10, 14, 142
Real Majority: An Extraordinary Examination of the Electorate, The, 153n1
Rebellion and Repression, 145
Resurgence, 37
Revolution for the Hell of It, 143
Ridgeway, James, 88, 145
Rock and Roll Will Stand, 130
Rock Revolution, The, 129
Rock Story, The, 129
Rolling Stone, 31, 32, 127, 128–29, 130
Romm, Ethel Grodzins, 12, 14, 25
Romney, Hugh, 30, 31, 142
Roszak, Theodore, 11, 119, 130
Rubin, Jerry, 119, 143, 144
Rudd, Mark, 26, 123, 124

Sanders, Ed, 37, 39
San Francisco *Chronicle,* 30, 128
San Francisco *Examiner,* 28
San Francisco *Oracle,* 15, 19, 30, 40
Saturday Evening Post, 96
Scammon, Richard, 153n1
Scherr, Max, 17
Schoenfeld, Dr. Eugene, 17
Scholes, Robert, 62–63, 71, 83–84
Screw, 32, 33
SDS New Left Notes, 26
Seale, Bobby, 28, 29, 110
Seed, 15, 18
Seldes, George, 154n3
Selling of the President 1968, The, 88, 145
Shaw, Arnold, 129
Shaw, Peter, 71–72
Sinclair, Upton, 47, 87
60 Minutes, 151

Slouching Towards Bethlehem, 96–100

Snatch, 32

SNCC Newsletter, 26, 28

Snow, C. P., 159*n11*

Sometimes a Great Notion, 59

Sontag, Susan, 87, 89, 90–93, 104

South Hampton Illustrated Times, 36

Stafford, Peter, 31

Stock, Dennis, 142

Stone, Chuck, 156*n5*

Stone, I. F., 4–7, 154*n3*

Stop-Time, 164*n9*

Strawberry Statement: Notes of a College Revolutionary, The, 121–24

Stuart, Lyle, 9

Student as Nigger, The, 121

Student Nonviolent Coordinating Committee (SNCC), 12, 26

Students for a Democratic Society (SDS), 12, 26, 39, 121, 123, 124

Supernation at Peace and War, 93–95

Talese, Gay, 50, 158–59*n2*

Tarbell, Ida M., 87

Tell It Like It Is, 156*n5*

Terkel, Studs (Louis), 96

Thompson, Hunter, 83, 131–33, 134, 135, 138

Time, 47, 69, 94–95, 139

Tribe, 17

Trip to Hanoi, 90–93, 104

Turning On, 134, 139–42

underground FM radio, 127–29, 151–52

underground newspapers, collections of, 157*n14*

Underground Press in America, The, 155*n6*

Underground Press Syndicate (UPS), 5, 6, 15–16, 18–19, 20, 29, 35, 37, 38, 48, 154*n6*

Unsafe at Any Speed, 144, 145

US, 9, 37, 38, 39

Vanocur, Sander, xvi

Village Voice, 7–17 *passim*, 77, 130, 137

von Braun, Werner, 81

von Hoffman, Nicholas, 97, 134–36, 137

Wakefield, Dan, 83, 87, 93–96, 97

Wallace, Henry, 26

War and Peace in the Global Village, 25, 45

Washington *Afro-American*, 156*n5*

Washington *Free Press*, 69

Washington *Post*, 19, 30, 69, 77, 134

Watson, James D., 160*n11*

Wattenberg, Ben, 153*n1*

We Are the People Our Parents Warned Us Against, 97, 134–36

Wenner, Jann, 31, 128

Why Are We in Vietnam?, 64, 67, 87

Wilcock, John, 6–7, 16, 17, 18, 38

Wolf, Dan, 7

Wolfe, Tom, xi, xvi, 48, 50–62, 63, 64, 65, 74, 77, 83–98 *passim*, 124, 131, 133, 138, 150, 169*n5*

Women's Liberation, 33, 165*n13*

Woodstock Nation, 143

Working Press, The, 46

World Journal Tribune, 54

Zap, 32